Software Testing:

A Guide to Testing Mobile

Apps, Websites, and Games

By Mark Garzone

Copyright © 2014

Disclaimer

All the material contained in this book is provided for educational and informational purposes only. No responsibility can be taken for any results or outcomes resulting from the use of this material.

While every attempt has been made to provide information that is both accurate and effective, the author does not assume any responsibility for the accuracy or use/misuse of this information.

To Alan Turning, the father of computer science and AI.

Preface

Why another book on software testing? This book was motivated by the observation that most testing books focus on one aspect of testing. There are not too many books on the market which look at the whole area of testing in a broad presentation of manual testing, performance testing, and automation testing. This book is a comprehensive treatment of the subject from the viewpoint of a practioning tester. It covers the techniques and tools that a tester needs to know to do their job.

Table of Contents

Chapter 1: Start of Project Testing Preparation

Introduction

What is practical software testing? It is a testing approach for quickly finding and reporting software defects based on practical testing experience. There are many books on the market covering traditional approaches to software testing. This book, unlike them, provides practical tips to running tests quickly at every stage of the software lifecycle. Let's not waste any more time and get on with it.

Beginning Phrase of Project

If you are invited to participate in the project from the very beginning you then have some time to do preparations which will save you time during the testing phase of the project. This is true for all types of software development models whether it be Agile, regular Waterfall, or the V model Waterfall variant. There are special situations in which the software development model is specified as for example when developing medical devices. In this case developers and tester must follow the processes defined in medical industry compliance regulations of FDA 21 or IEC 62304.

In agile testing before and during the beginning of the iteration you prepare for testing. In the regular Waterfall model the time for preparation is longer since testing starts only after code implementation. For the V model testing preparation occurs at each phase creating acceptance test cases for the requirements analysis phase, system test cases for the system requirement phase, integration test case for the module design phase, and unit test cases for the code implementation. Use your time wisely with good preparations to save time later during the test execution phase.

Tip #1

If your company is a startup or you are the first test manager at the company it is best to come up with a test strategy document. This document will not just be for your project but usually for all projects at your company and describe how testing is done at your company. A test strategy is the implementation of a test policy set by the IT management of a company. The test policy of a company will state things about testing such as all in-house developed code will be tested. A test strategy will include things like the following:

- Business issues
- Roles and responsibilities
- Communication and status reporting
- Test deliverability
- Industry standards to follow
- Test automation and tools
- Testing measurements and metrics
- Risks and mitigation
- Defect reporting and tracking
- Change and configuration management
- Training plan

Tip #2

Write a master test plan. A master test plan is a 1 to 3 pages document explaining briefly how the software is going to be tested. It should describe your test approach, the test data, the test environment, the test tools used and any assumptions, risks, and limitations you make about the testing of the software. This document is then shared with the stakeholders to get their feedback and clear up any misunderstandings. For instance it might say that performance testing is excluded. It might state that the testing will done on a particular environment, or a particular test data set is used, or what tools will be used.

Tip #3

Become an expert in the test domain. As they say "Knowledge is power" hence the more you know about the test domain the more powerful your testing will be. Preparation includes:

- Read the requirements document. If there is no requirements document, demand one even if the app is being developed by Agile. Maybe you will get one. Read whatever documentation there is available used in the design or building of the software. E.g. wireframes, Agile task boards, etc.

- Study the domain. If the software is going to be a dental billing software, study a little about book keeping and accounting and even dentist procedures. Look up and read up on the definitions of technical terms.

- If the product is going to be rewrite of existing software read any previous documentation on the product such as a user's manual.

- If the old software exists then run it and study how it works. Better still, ask the users of the existing software to give you a tour of the existing software. That way they can explain how things work and show what is important. This will be later helpful in prioritizing what to test in the regression tests.

⋏ Test competitor software that do the same thing as you application. This is a good way to get to know the domain and see how your application compares in terms of easy of use, and GUI look and feel.

Tip #4

Write high level test cases or test scenarios and ask lots of questions. If you have time before getting first version of the app write as many test cases as possible based on the requirements. The test cases do not necessarily need to be step-by-step detailed test cases. They can be high level test cases. Test cases are a good way to confirm your understanding of the software that you are going to test. You might not necessarily use them all during the tests due lack of time, requirements changing, etc. But by writing test cases you start to question "What does that requirement mean?" and "How can I test it?" Writing test cases allows you to form a plan of attack on the testing the validity of the implementation. If you don't understand what the requirement means then it's time to ask the requirements author or the customer for more details for clarification. When getting answers ask for specific examples or detailed answers. If something is missing, contradictory, or inconsistent then this should raise you red flag to ask questions.

The quickest way to write a high level tests that gets good coverage is to take each sentence in the requirements document and add the words "Test that...". For example if the requirement is that "All customer payments are made 30 days after the end of the month", then this is transformed into the following how level test case "Test that all customer payments are made 30 days after the end of the month." Do this for every sentence in the document. Now some sentences can be removed from the test plan as they might be duplicates of the content. Other long compound sentences with the conjunction words "and" and "or" can be split 2 or more high level test cases sentences.

These sentences are then added to your favorite test plan management tool such as TestLink. If you don't have one just create a spreadsheet with a minimum of 2 columns labeled "Test" and "Pass/Fail". Other columns that can be added are "Test Priority", "Comments", "Bug Ticket Number", "App Version", "Iteration",. Etc.

Tip #5

Use the eequivalence partitioning test technique when writing test cases to reduce the number of test cases required to test an input. It works by eliminating those redundant test cases that generate the same output and do not necessarily reveal defects in program functionality. For example testing a field that uses a 32 bit integer which takes values from -2,147,483,648 to 2,147,483,647 the equivalence test cases of -100, 0, and 100 covers all the negative numbers, the zero number, and the positive numbers. That is by partitioning the value space into 3 partitions and selecting a value from each of the partition sets, gives enough test cases to test all the values in the entire value space. This technique can be applied to other areas other than numbers.

Tip #6

Use a decision table (cause-and-effect table) to design test cases for complex set of inputs and action outputs. This technique aligns in a truth table with conditions on the left side, rules on the top, actions at the bottom together with the truth values of true and false (alternatively yes or no) in the table showing the relationships of the conditions, rules and actions. A rule is combination of the truth values for the conditions. Below is an example of a decision table for billing system,

Conditions	Rule 1,	Rule 2,	Rule 3
Payment is late	Y	Y	N
Payment is too small	Y	N	Y

Actions			
Send an email notice	Y	Y	N
Phone the customer	Y	N	Y

The test cases derived from this table would be the following:

1. Test that when the payment is late and payment is too small then an email notice is sent and the customer is phoned.

2. Test that when the payment is late then an email notice is sent.

3. Test that when the payment is too small then the customer is phoned.

Tip #7

Document each test case with the reference of the requirement that is being tested as a traceability matrix reference. Better still copy the requirement into the test case introduction section. That way you don't need to go looking up the original document to figure out the reason why you are testing that test case. Also it can be handy when doing change impact analysis to see quickly what needs to be regression tested when that requirement is changed.

Tip #8

Start preparations for required test materials and resources as soon as possible. You want to start preparations of setting up the all equipment and resources for testing to be done as early as possible, since unforeseen delays may occur and delay the start of your testing. Here are somethings you may want to consider getting done right away:

- Procure test equipment such as servers or mobile phones.

- Set up the test equipment.

- Request access to the test environment.

- Acquire the test data set. This might be a smaller sample from the live environment so somebody will have to spend time extracting it. If the test data is not derived from an existing source it will need to be generated which might take time to generate either by hand or by a program. Some projects do not require any special test data while other projects might need large data sets for performance testing. See the next section on more discussion on generating test data.

- Set up any special test tools.

- Request access to the test plan management software and bug defect tracking software.

- Establish contact with key persons such as support team, developers, customers, business analysts, project managers, etc. before the testing phrase so that time is not wasted in trying to get a hold of them when there is an urgent need to get answers or get requests done fast. Find out if any of them will be on vacation will you are running your tests. If so then ask who their replacements are while on vacation. There is nothing like trying to get a hold of someone on vacation who has not left a temporary point of contact while they are gone.

Test Effort Estimation

Don't estimate the testing effort unless it's absolutely mandatory. Testing usually stops when a deadline is reached and there is no much time or budget left to test. Alternatively testing stops when a quality condition is met such as all blocker and critical bugs are fixed.

If you are forced to estimate the testing effort then the estimate depends on the software development approach. If the approach is Agile then the testing time will be built into the agile iteration cycle. Hence this will be determined by the number of iterations. If you are doing a Waterfall model of testing then count the number of test cases created and multiple by X minutes per test cases to get a total test time for a 1 test run on the feature set. For calculating the time for retesting fixes multiple the number of estimated defects per feature by the number of minutes it takes you retest the feature. Also the regression test effort is the number of regression test cases selected multiplied by the number of minutes per test cases. The total testing effort is then the sum of those three numbers plus test support activities such test planning and test reporting. If automation or performance testing will be done then that needs to be added as well.

Total Time = Feature Testing Time + Retesting Fixes Time + Regression Testing Time + Test Support Activities

Another quick way to estimate the test time is to count the number of inputs and output of the requirements design screenshot or wireframe and multiple that by an average number of minutes it would take to test it. For instance if a requirements screenshot shows that the web page has 4 text fields, 3 dropdowns and 2 checkboxes then assuming it takes 15 minutes to test each widget it will take a total time of 7 x 15 = 75 minutes. Repeat this over the whole application and sum up the result for the total test time estimate.

Pair Design and Test

Pair programming is a technique of two programmers coding side by side. Pair design and test is when the business analyst and tester work together when a wireframe or screenshot has been created and not yet officially added to the requirements document. The tester identifies problems with the wireframe or screenshot to the designer who then fixes it. The advantage of this approach is that tester tells what the error is before the developer wrongly codes it into existence.

Chapter 2: Test Data Generation

Test data generation is an important part of testing as the quality and the quantity of test data determines in a large part the success of the testing effort. Here are some approaches to generating test data:

- Use directly a copy of live data from an existing application.

- Generate test data based on analysis of the live data to select a subset of values.

- Generate test data with random values. This is the simplest method for generating test data. It can be a string of random bit stream to represent a data type. Alternatively it can be a random selection of known values for each data row. Random test data generation does not generate quality test data as it does not perform well in terms of coverage.

- Generate test data based on test cases.

- Generate test data based on code coverage of paths in the program. For instance a program can be considered to have execution paths through the code based on the initial data input. A test generator will select a path to the program and then generate the test data that tests this path to find faults in it.

Once the approach is chosen a decision needs to be made in what format is the data to be stored. The test data can be stored in CVS files, XML files, Excel spreadsheets, properties files, or in a database.

Next the amount of data needs to be determined for running tests. For performance tests use large data sets that match as closely as possible the expected database size in the production environment. If test execution modifies or deletes the data, remember to backup a copy of the data so that test data can reverted back to the initial state quickly.

Test Data Generation Tools

Besides coding a program to generate test data or using an Excel macro there are online websites for generating test data and test data generator tools such below to help with this task:

- ⅄ Check out the websites for generating random test data such as www.databasetestdata.com or www.generatedata.com . See Figure 1.

- ⅄ SQL Data Generator by Red Gate is a fast tool for creating realistic test data. This tool provides generators based on table and column names, field length, and data types. They can be adjusted to meet your requirements, and include a scriptable Python generator.

- ⅄ GS Data Generator is an automated testing and data generation tool, which creates random test data for performance testing, usability testing and database load testing.

- ⅄ IRI RowGen is a tool whose major strengths are fast generation of billions of sorted rows, random data generation from metadata, and preservation of referential integrity of the data generated.

- ⅄ Datanamic Data Generator MultiDB is a powerful data generator that allows programmers with easy to populate databases with thousands of rows of test data for DB testing purposes. Other features include: populating database directly or generate insert scripts, data generation based on column characteristics, and customization of data generators.

⅄ EMS Data Generator for SQL Server is a powerful tool for generating test data to SQL Server DB tables. The scripts can be saved and edited.

⅄ Data Generator is a utility to populate, create and load tables with semi random data. This utility allows users to specify sequences, random text, random numbers, database columns and files as sources for tables.

⅄ Databene Benerator is a framework for generating high-volume test data. Benerator supports the following formats: XML, XML Schema, CSV, flat files and Excel sheets. Domain packages provide reusable generators for creating domain-specific data as names and addresses customized by language and region.

⅄ DTM Data Generator Overview is a tool that makes data rows, tables, views, procedures for DB testing purposes.

⅄ Advanced Data Generator Series is a set of test data generator tools which creates fake but realistic data quickly for databases.

⅄ Spawner is a generator tool of test data for databases. This tool can be configured to output delimited text or SQL insert statements for insert directly into a MySQL database. It includes many field types which are configurable. See Figure 2.

⅄ IBM DB2 Test Database Generator is an add-on tool for DB2 that helps programmers speedily create test data from nothing or from existing data.

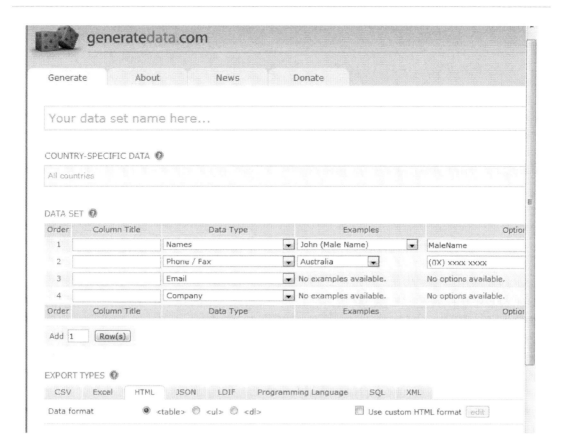

Figure 1

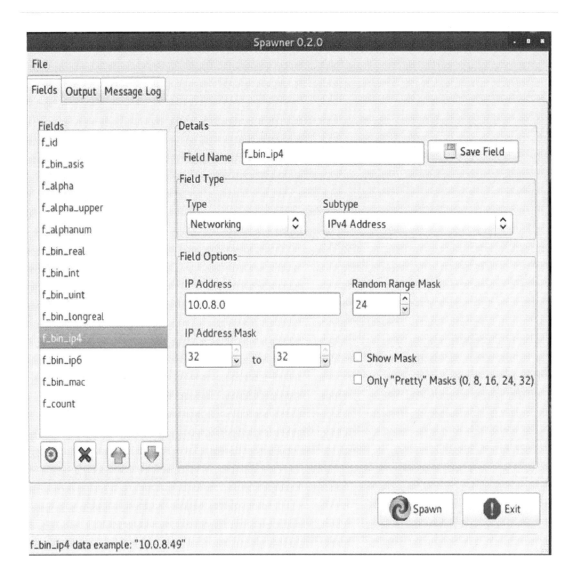

Figure 2

Chapter 3: Development Testing Phase of the Project

The first release of the software is ready for testing and you are ready to go. The testing phase activities are dependent on timeline demands. Typically the testing phrase is divided into several test cycles that happen after every version release. The order of testing activities that should be done is from most important to least important. Here's the test cycle outline for two different types of projects.

Test Cycle of Medium Length Project (total project time up to 4 months).

1. Run new features test cases.

2. While waiting for fixes, run exploratory testing.

3. Retest fixes.

4. Run regression test cases.

5. Send testing status email to project manager on a weekly/monthly/iteration basis.

6. Plan and update test cases for next test cycle iteration.

7. Start writing other test related documentation such as the test exit report.

Test Cycle of Long Length Project (total project time > 4 months)

1. Run new features test cases.

2. While waiting for fixes, run exploratory testing.

3. Retest fixes.

4. Run regression test cases.

5. Run automated tests if created for long projects.

6. Create new automated test cases.

7. Send email for the testing status to project manager on a weekly/monthly/iteration basis.

8. Plan and update test cases for next test cycle iteration.

9. Start writing other test related documentation such as the test exit report.

Remember the goal of testing is to find bugs and report them to the developers so that they can fix them. Anything else like test reports don't necessarily help in finding the bugs in the software. They might be important for others such as the project manager or shareholders but not necessarily to your job as the finder of defects, hence they take the least priority.

If the project has performance requirements then an additional test cycle is added at the end of the project to test that the application meets those requirements.

Tip # 8

Ask the developer to demo and explain the features implemented for a release. This gives the tester an opportunity to ask questions about the version being demonstrated. If you are lucky bugs will appear during the demo. There's nothing like the developer finding bugs for you and saving you testing effort.

Pair Code and Test

Pair programming is a technique of two programmers coding side by side. Pair code and test is when the programmer and tester work side by side for a short session when a feature is being implemented and not yet checked in officially into the source code release. The tester can for instance check a screen and in person or over a chat report anything wrong with the GUI to the developer. The advantage of this approach is that tester tells the developer what the bug is without writing a ticket and the developer fixes the bug right away if simple. This saves time. After the short pair session the tester can retest the feature in greater depth.

Test Scenarios Give Lighting Fast Test Plans

Planning your tests is an important activity. Often a looming deadline puts the test team in a race for time so writing a full blown test suite of test cases with detailed steps and expected results can put the testing team behind schedule. How does a test team handle such a situation? The answer is write test scenarios.

What exactly is a test scenario? Well it can be thought of a high level test case without all the details of a test case. It tests a particular scenario of the application. The definition of a scenario from the Collins English dictionary is "sequence of events, chain of events, course of events, series of developments".

The best place to find test scenarios is the use cases specified in the requirements document. So how does a test scenario compare to a test case? Let's take for example the user case of a user logging into the application successfully. The test scenario corresponding to this would be:

"Test that the user logins successfully into the application with their correct username and password".

Compare that to the detailed step-by-step test case which takes 5 times longer to write.

1. Type the home page www.website.com in the browser url field

2. Click on login link labelled "Login here".

3. Type the username johnsmith1 in the Username field.

4. Type the password "ABC2Tz@" in the Password field.

5. Click the login button labelled "Submit"

So the next time your test team is behind schedule write test scenarios instead of long detailed test cases to save time. Your project manager will praise you to making lost time.

Chapter 4: Regression Testing

What is regression testing? Regression testing is running tests to make sure no bugs are introduced into existing tested software as a result of a change of the software. One option for regression testing is to re-run all test cases. This is required for mission critical safety application whose potential could endanger life and property such as a nuclear plant. For most other apps not all test cases need to be re-run to save time. Thus the issue of building a regression test suite becomes what test cases should be selected for a regression test run. Here are some approaches to regression testing:

- Main workflow use cases. Select test cases which test highly used features. This is a good approach since it concentrates finding bugs in areas of the application that are important to the user by virtue of it being used often. This often the preferred approach since the defects which are not found during the regression tests will be eventually discovered by the users as the users will use those high used features.

- High risk areas of software. Select more high risk test cases whose impact of failure is high. For instance test the payment system for a web app store application. If the purchase system fails than the website will not make money and potentially go bankrupt. This is a high risk test case.

- Impacted code analysis of software. Select test cases whose code could be impacted by a change. For instance changing a DB table definition might break all the code that uses that table. Hence run test cases that touch that DB table. This approach is theoretically the optimal approach since it tests only the changed areas and their dependencies minimizing regression testing effort. The only problem with this approach is that it is hard to identify what dependencies are of the initial feature changes. For instance customer data used in customer profile form might be used in many places in the application. Testing the original code change in the customer form is easy but tracking where the customer data is used in the application is hard without resorting to code analysis tools.

⋏ Statistical sampling. Select test cases using statistical sampling theory. This is an excellent approach but requires the tester to have statistics training. For further discussion on this approach see the article by "Software Reliability Assessment by Statistical Analysis of Operational Experience" by Sven Söhnlein and Francesca Saglietti.

⋏ Weighted sampling based components age. Select more test cases of newer components which are less tested than older components which have been already tested many times.

⋏ Weighted sampled based on components bug density. Select more test cases for components that are unstable and have more defects than other components.

How does one go about identifying highly used features for selecting test cases that test them? Do the following:

⋏ Consult the requirements document or the business analyst who wrote it.

⋏ Ask the users what features they use most often.

⋏ Analyze the usage analytics data. This is the best way since it is based on the tracking of real user behaviour and not on opinions nor predictions of user behaviour. Often there is no usage analytics data collected so data mining needs to be conducted on the database and server logs. For websites installing Google analytics hooks gives a simple fast way to see page usage, browser usage, and OS usage. For desktop applications there are monitoring software tools such as OpenSpan Desktop Analytics which can provide this usage data.

Regression test suite management is a key activity of test managers and testers. Putting significant thought into this activity finds more relevant bugs during the regression test cycle and gets more bang out of the regression test suite.

Chapter 5: Test Plan Management Tools

Unless you are planning not to write test cases for test plans it is highly recommended that you use a test plan management tool. Here's a list of good test planning tools most of which are open source. Why play for a tool when it's free unless it is offers something extra useful? Use the money instead for something else like more pizza for testers.

- ⚔ Quality Spy is a good lightweight test management tool alternative to the other existing heavy tools.

- ⚔ Klaros Test Management is a professional, web based test management tool which has components for planning and evaluating test activities. Test requirements tracking is supported as well as agile methodologies such as like Scrum or Kanban. There is also a mobile edition which allows testers to concentrate on the testing task without having to work on complex test management software.

- ⚔ TestRail is a slick test management in which statistics and activity charts are built-in and are always visible,

- ⚔ TestLink is a test management tool which has great built-in reports and access to data. To integrate with external bug tracking system additional tools need to be build or purchased. See Figure 3.

- ⚔ Tarantula is fantastic tool for managing software testing in agile software projects. Tarantula is free to use under the open source license GNU GPLv3. See Figure 4.

- ⚔ XStudio is a leading ALM solution that covers the complete life-cycle of your testing projects from beginning to end:

products/releases, requirements, specifications, agile projects, tests, test campaigns, test reports and defects. There are three versions with a free community version. See Figure 5.

- Testopia is a test case management extension for Bugzilla for tracking test cases. Testopia allows testers to attach bugs to test case run results for centralized management of the software engineering process within Bugzilla.

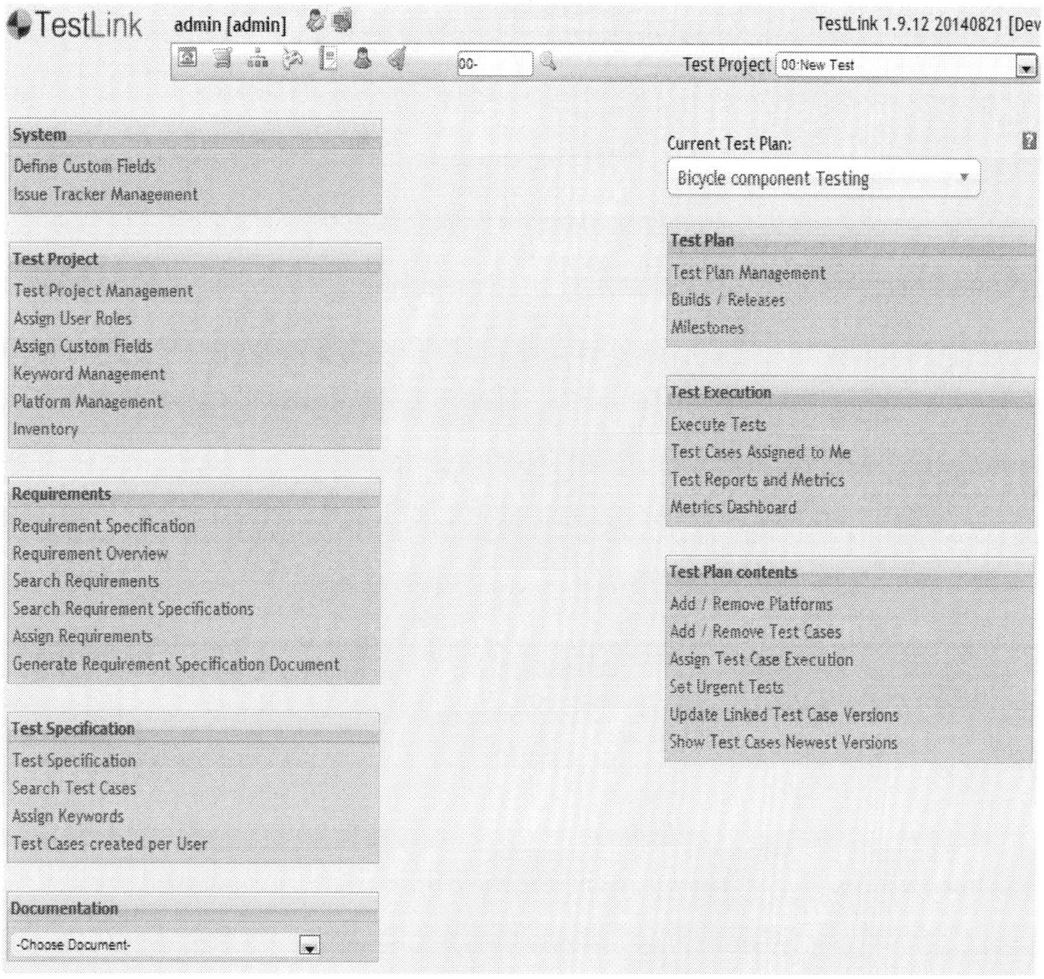

Figure 3

Figure 4

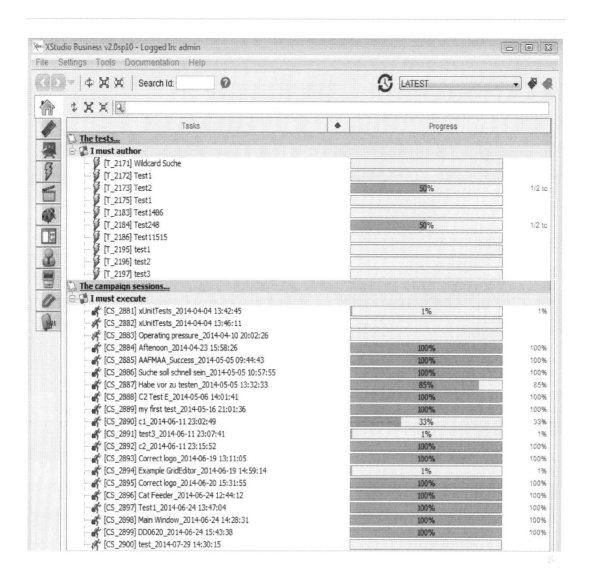

Figure 5

Chapter 6: Bug Reporting Tools

Unless you are the only tester sitting beside the only programmer and can interrupt their work day constantly with "Hey Mister Developer, got a moment? I found another bug. Check this out..." you need a bug reporting tool to track bugs or issues found. Again go with the open source bug reporting tool to save money. However there are some paid tools that are worth looking into if you are not a startup and short of funds.

- ⅄ Bugzilla is probably the most popular web-based bug tracker and testing tool originally developed and used by the Mozilla project. Features include time tracking, integrated email capabilities, flexible reporting and charting, customized fields and workflows. See Figure 6.

- ⅄ MantisBT is another popular web-based bug tracking system built on PHP. Features include source code integration, time tracking, issue relationship graph, custom fields and workflow. See Figure 7.

- ⅄ Trac is an enhanced wiki and issue tracking system for software development projects. Trac integrates into Subversion and Git and has good reporting facilities. See Figure 8.

- ⅄ Redmine is written in Ruby on Rails for tracking issues. It also provides a full project management features. Features include, project management including Gantt chart, wiki, time tracking, and LDAP Authentication.

- ⅄ Request Tracker is a time-tested issue tracking system which many organizations use for bug tracking, help desk ticketing, customer service, and workflow processes.

⅄ OTRS is an open-source trouble ticket system software package that a company can utilized to assign tickets to incoming queries and track further communications about them. Managed OTRS is the paid cloud-based version of the system if you are not interested in the hassle of maintaining the system on your servers.

⅄ The Bug Genie is bug tracker and project management tool. It has project dashboards. The bugs are easy to find with a filter and the search results can be groups and saved. A wiki package is built into the tool.

⅄ JIRA is a tracking bug and project management tool which allows you to schedule milestones, activities, and track employee time. There are dashboards along with query and reporting of issues. JIRA has lots of add-ons which plug into the tool.

There are many other bug tracking tools to list and go over. Do some research on the following, FogBugz, IBM Rational ClearQuest, Lighthouse, Zoho bug tracker, BugHost, BugNET, eTraxis, and HP Application Lifecycle Management.

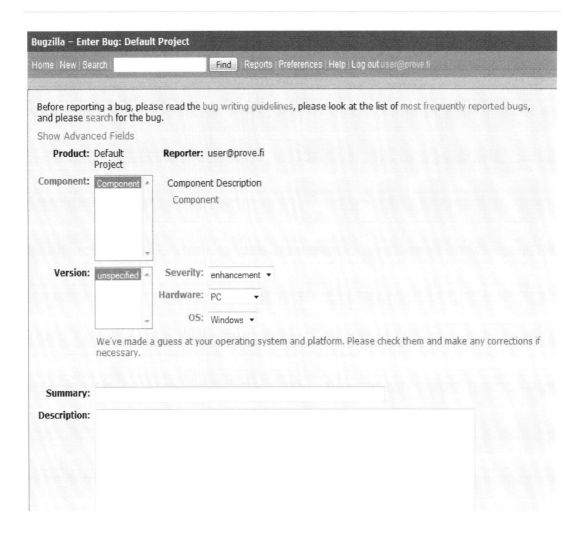

Figure 6

Figure 7

Create New Ticket

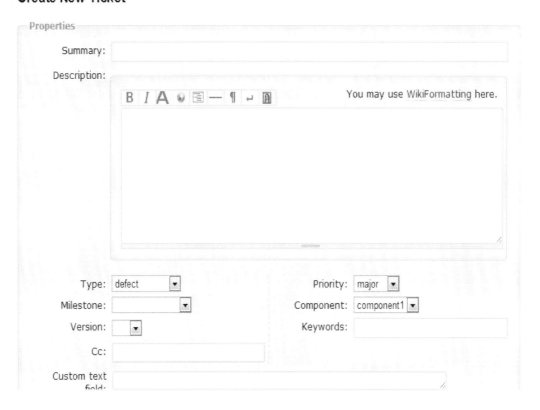

Figure 8

Chapter 7: Test Metrics

A test metric is a measure of an attribute related to testing. Test metrics are important since they can used to quantify the current state of testing. Based on information steps can be taken to improve the testing process, or take action based on the current testing status to remedy any problems that the metrics indicate. There are two types of metrics; base metrics and calculated metrics. Base metrics are a direct measure of some part of testing such as the number of test cases executed. Calculated metrics are functions of base metrics. For example the calculated metric % test cases completed = (test cases run / total number of test cases.) x 100. Below some more common calculated metrics.

Test Plan Coverage on Functionality = (No of requirements covered / total number of requirements) x 100

Thus test plan coverage = (100/200) x 100 = 50%

Test case defect density = (number of test cases failed / number of test case run) x 100.

Example: Total test script developed 1360, total test script executed 1280, total test script passed 1065, and total test script failed 215

Thus the test case defect density is (215/1280) X 100 = 16.8%

Defect slippage ratio = (Customer filed defects / Number of valid defects raised) x 100

Example: Customer filed defects are 21, total defect found while testing are 267, total number of invalid defects are 17

Therefore, Slippage Ratio is [21/(267-17)] X 100 = 8.4%

Requirement Volatility = (Number of Requirements Added + Deleted + Modified) x100 / Number of Original Requirements

Example: Version 1 had total 67 requirements initially, later they added another 7 new requirements and removed 3 from initial requirements and modified 11 requirements

So, requirement Volatility is (7 + 3 + 11) * 100/67 = 31.3%

Review efficiency=100*Total number of defects found by reviews/Total number of project defects

Example: A project found total 269 defects in different reviews, which were fixed and test team got 476 defects which were reported and valid

So, Review efficiency is [269/(269+476)] X 100 = 36.1%

Defect Severity Index = (4 x number blocker bugs + 3 x number critical bugs + 2 x number major bugs + 1 x number of minor bugs) / Total number of defects

Example: : A project at the last testing iteration has a total 62 defects broken down by 2 blockers, 10 criticals, 20 majors + 30 minors.

So, defect severity index is [2x4+ 10x3+ 2x20+30x1] = 1.7

Defects/KLOC = Number of defects / thousand lines of code

Example 60 bugs /10,000 lines = 6 bugs/KLOC

Sometimes the number of lines of code is not known by the tester so assuming that the programmer roughly codes the same amount of code per day we get another metric of Defects/number of coding days = 500/83 coding days = 6 bugs/code day.

Tip #33

When starting to use testing metrics introduce them one by one into your organization. Focus on the most problematic testing metric and once the problem which the metric measures is under control introduce the next metric. This divide and conquer strategy will prevent the management from being overwhelmed with information overload provided by the all the testing metrics used at once. You track all metrics privately in a dashboard and just bring to attention the ones that are most urgent for action.

Chapter 8: Automation Testing

Automation testing is using software to run tests without manual intervention on the software being tested. This testing is hard coded, based on recorded scripts or based on programmed scripts. The benefits of automation testing is that once a test is automated it can be run many times automatically without using expensive tester resources. This can lead to potential significant savings if the setup costs are less than the number of times the automated tests are run. To be more precise the formula for determining if automation is worthwhile is the following when left side cost > right side cost

Number of Scripts x (Number of Test Runs per script x Manual Tester Cost Saved by Script) > Number of Automation Scripts x (Coding Cost per Script) + Cost of Tool

For tools that do not need any scripting like web broken link parser or web security parser then the formula becomes:

Number of Test Runs x Manual Tester Cost Saved by Test Run > Cost of Tool

If the cost of the tool is free due to it being open source then it's a no brainer to automate these tests.

All manual testing cannot be automated since there are certain types of testing that a machine cannot do such as testing userability and GUI look and feel inconsistencies in the application. It is best to automate the regression test suite to have it run automatically part as the automated build center. After each automatic build the failed test results are emailed to the testers for further investigation. Once the failure is confirmed as an error a bug ticket can be reported.

Automation testing can be done for different types of testing. Often white box testing is automated at the unit level and integration level. Developers are responsible for writing unit tests when doing test driven development (TDD). These tests can run when the code is checked into the source code control system or in an automated build center on a schedule. Sometimes the programmers are too busy to write unit tests or integration tests and then a tester writes them.

UI Automated Testing Tools

Below are some commonly used tools for GUI automated testing tools used in automation testing.

- Selenium is a well-known open-source tool for Web UI automation testing. Selenium has a GUI IDE for recording and playing back test cases. See Figure 9. Also there is a selenium web driver that can be programmed and run as JUnit test cases. See Figure 10. Selenium's web automation scripts must be programmed in one of the following languages of Java, C#, Python, Ruby, Perl, or PHP. Selenium requires an understanding of HTML, CSS and JavaScript since element selectors need to be coded for finding a particular GUI widget to test for a condition. Firebug, a browser plugin, is helpful here for identifying these selectors.

⋏ Sikuli is another open-source test automation tool that locates anything from the screen, based on image recognition techniques. It is useful when there is no easy access to a GUI's internal or source code such as desktop apps. Sikuli uses Python and Java as a scripting language and makes use of the screenshots for GUI automation tests. See Figure 11.

⋏ AutoIt v3 is a freeware BASIC-like scripting language designed for automating the Windows GUI and general scripting. It uses a combination of simulated keystrokes, mouse movement and window/control manipulation in order to automate tasks in a way not possible or reliable with other languages. See Figure 12.

⋏ TestComplete provides an open test platform for easily scripting automated tests for desktop, web, mobile, and client-server software application. TestComplete's recorder records tests for your Android apps.

⋏ TestStack White is a framework for automating rich client applications based on Win32, WinForms, WPF, Silverlight and SWT platforms. Automation programs using White can be scripted with any .NET language. White provides a consistent object-oriented API, hiding the complexity of Microsoft's UIAutomation library (on which White is based) and windows messages. A recorder is no longer provided, so it is recommended testers have programming skills.

⋏ HP QuickTest Professional (QTP) is an easy to use, premium automated functional testing tool that helps testers to perform automated regression testing. Test scripts are programmed in VBScript. It is integrated with many other resources for testing.

⊼ UIA Verify is a test automation framework that features the User Interface Automation Test Library and Visual UI Automation Verify, the graphical user interface tool. This is an open source project by Microsoft and the successor to UI Spy.

Tip #9

Use the Selenium IDE to record all of our test cases then export it "Java / JUnit 4 / Webdriver" and run it in WebDriver with Eclipse. It is not a 100% reliable but it will save you a lot a time creating the test cases from scratch.

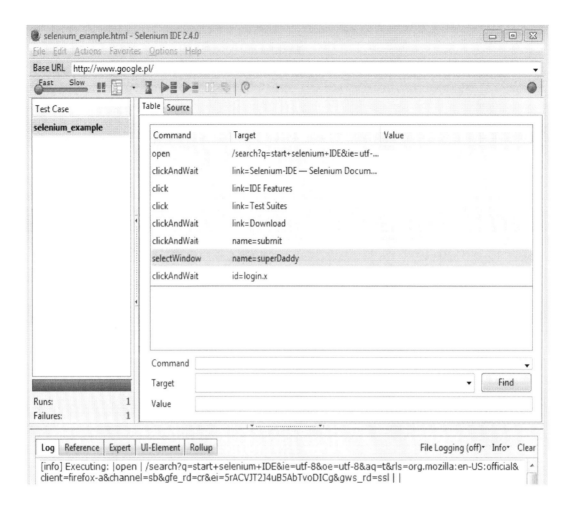

Figure 9

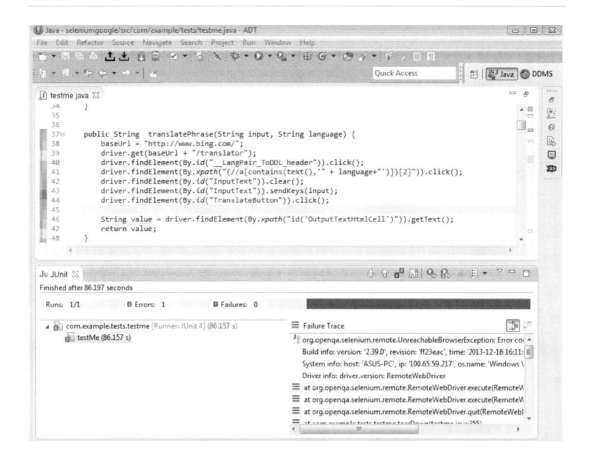

Figure 10

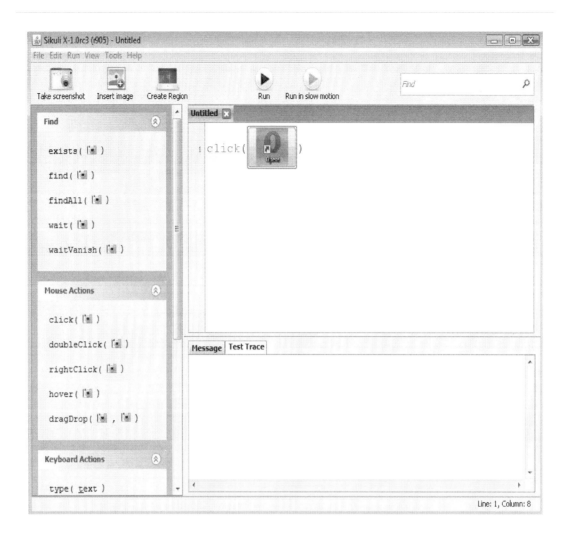

Figure 11

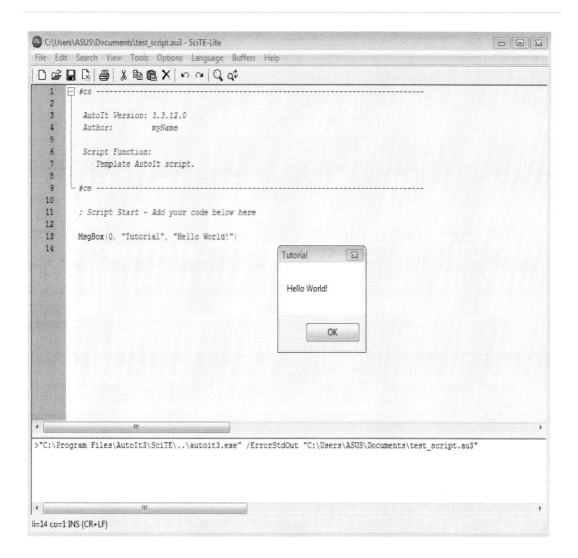

Figure 12

Chapter 9: Exploratory Testing

Exploratory testing is running tests without written test cases. The test cases are synthesized in the mind of the tester during the actual testing based on the tester's experience and intuition. The power of exploratory testing is that the tester does not need to stick to the original test plan which might be incomplete due to lack of time, outdated, or not thought of during the time the test cases were created.

Tip #10

It is best to have more than one tester execute an exploratory testing session. By having more than one tester test the software it brings another set of eyes, experience and their equipment into detecting the errors. If there is only one tester per project have the testers switch between the projects temporarily for one exploratory testing session.

Tip #11

Ask the business analysts do exploratory testing. They often see functional defects that are not in the well written sections of the requirement docs

Tip #12

Invite users to do exploratory testing before the release. They know what they want. Also they should ideally do the acceptance testing.

Tip #13

Use crowd testing to do exploratory testing. If having another tester run exploratory testing is good, having hundreds of crowd testers do exploratory testing will be better and find more bugs. This of course costs money. A cheaper alternative to crowd testing is to have a bug finding contest company wide and offer prizes for the top bug finders. A popular crowd testing portal is uTest for all types of apps. Mob4hire is good for mobile app crowd testing.

Tip #14

Use a checklist of software bug attacks to guide your exploratory testing. This will remind you of all the possibilities that you can test while running your exploratory tests. See the list of test heuristics used to attack software in this book. Alternatively to a using a checklist, consult the bug reporting tool and look that the bug tickets reported for a similar type of project by the same programmers that are on the current project. Often the same type of bugs is created by the same programmers on the new project. Programmers are slow to change their programming ways and often repeat the same types of errors from project to project.

Tip #15

Consider doing a session based exploratory testing session. This special exploratory session is one in which the goal of the session is defined as a charter beforehand and the results are officially recorded. For instance you might want to focus on security type tests as your goal during an exploratory testing session.

Tip #16

When doing exploratory testing it is good to have the requirements document open to quickly reference any description of the behavior or appearance of the application and compare it to what you observe.

Where to Start an Exploratory Testing Session?

Deciding where to start exploratory testing an application is a key decision that determines the success of finding defects for a given test session.

Here are some starting entry points to consider:

- features which are new. New features often are under tested by test cases.

- features with few or no test cases in the test plan. These are ripe areas since the lack of test cases usually means under testing.

- features not included in the regression test plan. Perhaps they broke in the last change release and were missed due to the regression test plan not covering them.

- features which users complain about being buggy or awkward to use. Check the support help desk emails or talk to the users to uncover the buggy areas of the software.

- features with high defect density or defect rich hot spots. This indicates the code is poorly written and probably has more hidden defects

- features lacking requirements or have poorly written

requirements. Programmers end up doing their own thing which might be inconsistent with the overall design.

↟ features with low number of unit tests coverage. Basic errors caught by such unit tests usually slip thru without them.

↟ features with high code complexity. Studies have shown a high correlation between cyclomatic complexity and their faultiness

↟ features coded by an inexperienced junior programmer. They usually don't have enough coding experience often missing proper error handling code.

↟ features already tested by a junior tester. They don't have enough tester experience to pick up all the defects.

Chapter 10: Test Heuristics to Attack Software

Every tester needs a war chest of tricks to uncover bugs. Here is a list of software attack techniques to find bugs which can be used on a variety of software.

Requirements Attack

Test that the requirements are implemented. Look up the definitions of any technical terms and check what the valid values are for that technical term. Check also that the definitions of even non-technical difficult words are correctly interpreted in the implementation of the requirements. Developers who implement the requirements might have a different understanding of a word than what the author intended who used it in defining the requirement.

Empty Values/Default Values Attack

Test that field is able to handle empty values, blanks, and default values correctly.

Too Big/Long Attack

Test that the field is able to handle a too big value or too long string, too long file name. E.g. 99999999999999999999999999999

Too Small/Short Attack

Test that the field is able to handle a too small value or too short string.

For instance if the field is an integer test that it handles -999999999999999 correctly. For string fields test that it is able to handle blank spaces correctly.

Duplicate Values Attack

Test that adding the same value twice which violates uniqueness constraints is handled properly.

Special Characters Values Attack

Test that the field is able to handle special values correctly. E.g. " ' ` | / \ , ; : & < > ^ * ? Tab €, £

Boundary Values Attack

Test that the field is able to handle boundary values correctly. E.g. if boundary value is 5, test that it behaves correctly for 4, 5, and 6. That is boundary value -1, boundary value, and boundary value +1.

Chinese Characters Values Attack

Test that a string field is able to handle Chinese/Russian/Arabic and or accented characters.

Invalid Format Values Attack

Test that field is able to handle invalid formatted data. E.g. the American date field format is MM/DD/YYYY while in some European countries it is DD.MM.YYYY. E.g. an American number field uses commas as separator and a period as decimal point while the

European format is commas for decimal point and period or space for separator. 1,000.99 vs 1 000,99 Other examples include scientific notation, email format, and phone number format e.g. 1-(491)-556-4556

Security Vulnerability Attack

Test that field is able to handle security attack such as SQL injection, JavaScript injection, cross script injection, buffer overflow array out of bounds error. Most of these tests can be executed via security vulnerability detection tools.

Simultaneous Concurrent Usage Attack

Test that system is able to handle concurrent changes on a record by two users/operations . The application should be able to handle concurrent operations or show the correct error.

Interruption Attack

Test that the system is able to handle an interruption such a loss of internet connection. Other interruptions include application killed, server killed, DB stopped, computer turned off, app closed before sequence of operations is finished to complete an atomic action.

Stop and Resume Attack

Test that the system is able to handle stopping and resuming an operation. For example test stopping the application while an object is in an incomplete state or an action is in-progress, and then restarting the application again and resuming the processing of an incomplete state object or action.

Heavy Load Attack

Test that the system is able to handle too much load attack. An example of this is many users using this, or a very big data file being uploaded.

Very Long Attack

Test that the system is able to handle a very long running app attack. Running an operation or application non-stop over a long period such over the weekend might show defects related to out of memory, or out of disk space if the clean-up code is not properly coded.

Below Minimum Requirements Attack

Test that the system is able to gracefully handle being run on a platform or environment which it is not designed to work in. It should detect this case and show an error message and close. To create platforms which you do not have on your computer use Oracle's VirtualBox to create virtual machines with a specified OS to test various minimum OS configurations. VirtualBox is a powerful x86 and AMD64/Intel64 virtualization product for enterprise as well as home use which runs on various OS hosts. See Figure 13.

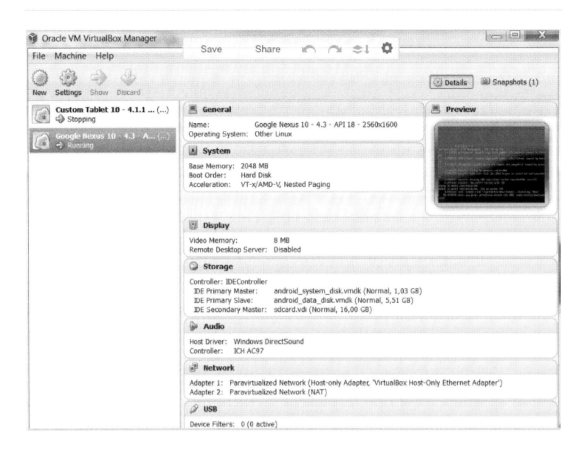

Figure 13

Low Resources Attack

Test that the system is able to gracefully handle run on a low resource environment due to it being taken by other programs. E.g. low memory, low hard disk space, high CPU utilization. It should detect this case and show an error message and close.

Time Dependencies Attack

Test that the system is able to handle the wrong time for a time dependent operation. Examples of this are wrong client/server computer time, wrong locale time, wrong future date, wrong past date, daylight saving time, and end of day, month or year change.

Compatibility Attack

Test that the system is able to run on various platforms. Examples of this include different browsers, operating systems, and hardware. Often errors occur with the older versions which are not compatible with the latest software frameworks. Also there is sometimes the problem of the current software not working with the latest hardware and or software which will be release soon. Try to get the beta version of the newest hardware/software and test on it.

Bad Configuration Attack

Test that the system is able to handle with the wrong configuration values. Configurations are either in a file or in a database. Change these values to bad values and test that the system is able to detect and deal gracefully with this.

Data Flow Components Attack

Test that the data that is entered or updated in one place flows correctly throughout the application various components and GUI views all the way to the intended external output. Make sure it is transformed in any erroneous way. Try entering very big values to see if it leads to errors as the data flows through the various interfaces of the system. Think of this test as dropping a ball down the drain. The ball might get stuck flowing through the different smaller pipes if the ball is too big. Look up the defect list of any frameworks, and 3rd party components used in the app and then attack those weaknesses.

Relationship Dependency Attack

Test that all relationship dependencies are not violated by using the application. For instance in a family tree application this would be trying to add two biological mothers for a single child. This is an error since a child can only have one biological mother. Sometimes the dependencies are indirect. Try to create circular dependencies or self-dependencies and check how the application handles those situations.

Repeated Operation Attack

Test that repeating the same operation many times is handled properly. For instance double click on the same button quickly. Another example is deleting the same item twice.

Recursive Objects Attack

Test that embedding an object within another object recursively. E.g. a diagram with an embedded diagram containing another diagram, etc.

Spelling, Punctuation, and Grammar Attack

Test that the application is correct for spelling, punctuation, and grammar. Often titles or headers are incorrectly capitalized.

Inconsistency Attack

Test that the application is consistent for look-and-feel, operations, actions, and error messages through all the GUI of the application.

Usability Attack

Test that the application is easy-to-use and intuitive. Although this is not a defect you can be sure that if the application is hard to use for a professional tester it will be hard to use for an average user. This should be raised as an improvement ticket unless the application is not usable due to that bad design. Things to test for usability include the following:

- Too small font size or too large font size.

- Bad color contrast combinations between text and background. E.g. Red text on blue ground or green text on red background is hard to read. Also low contrast is not good too like light green text on dark green background. Also about 8% population has color blindness and certain color combinations such as green text on red background or red text on green background cannot be read.

- Buttons that are too small and too hard to click on.

- Dropdown boxes that are too short to show the full text of items

- Too deep navigation to find page to do action

- Too much information on a page. Experts believe that human mind can hold approximately 7 items in short-term memory for about 20 to 30 seconds. Try to limit the number of elements on the page to 7 labels/buttons/fields so the page is not too cluttered and information overloaded.

- Missing help tips.

Permutations Attack

Test that an action that is dependent on a sequence of operations is able to handle the action done in different permutation sequence of operations. For instance if action is A, B, C, D → E, it handles the action for B, A, C, D → E. The number of permutations for arranging n operations is n!. For instance 3 operations A, B, C would be 3! = 3 x 2 x 1 = 6. That is ABC, ACB, BAC, BCA, CAB, and CBA. The permutations attack can be applied to the sequence of input data values.

Combinations Attack

Test that an action that is dependent on a data set irregardless of the order is able to handle the action done in a different combination of data. The number of combinations of n objects taken r at a time is $n!/[(n - r)! \times r!]$. E.g. group of 2 fields out of 3 fields A, B, C with values combination is $3!/[(3 - 2)!\ 2!] = 6/[(1)\ 2] = 3 = AB, AC, BC$. The combinations attack can be applied to the set of operations.

File Attack

Test that app is able to handle when the app's file is locked by another application. Also test that the app is able to handle when the app's file is deleted accidently while in use.

Internationalization and Localization Attack

Test that the text descriptions are not too long for labels, buttons and other GUI elements when the locale is changed. Make sure all elements are translated and not hard coded in the program. Test that dates and numerical values, currency are in the correct locale format. Make sure that images with text are localized. Check that the fonts, character encoding and text size is okay for the target language.

Grey Box Attack

Using knowledge about the underlying algorithm and data structures from documentation, or looking that the code design, run functional tests based on this insight on how the application works. For instance if you can look at the DB structure and see that the column of the table for username is 20 characters try entering a username with 30 characters and see if able to handle this situation. Another example would be if a recursive function is used for an algorithm to compute something, try a long enough value to cause a stack overflow.

Compliance Attack

Test that the software adheres to any regulations required for accessibility, privacy and legal standards specific to the field. For example banks are supposed to comply with regulations for FFEIC, FATCA, and Dodd Frank. Review the regulations and then design tests to check if the application meets those regulations.

Chapter 11: End Testing Phase of the Project

After completing the development testing phase of the project there are still activities left to finish off the project. These include:

1. Retest fixes from user accepting testing or beta testing.

2. Test deployment procedures in a reference test environment. Test the back out to previous version in case the new version fails for whatever reason. The nothing worst the having to back out the newly deployed version without a back out plan to revert to the previous version.

3. Regression test and system test the application in the reference environment.

4. Smoke test the application in the live production environment.

5. Complete writing any test related documentation such as the test exit report.

6. Hold a post project evaluation meeting to discuss what worked and what did not work.

Tip #17

Double check that all features in the requirements are implemented to prevent an app being deployed with missing features. Go line by line in the requirements document and compare to the app to see if the feature is there. You are not checking to see if the feature works just that it is present. When the application is nearly completed anything not implemented yet must be reported as a ticket to remind the developers to finish off any missing functionality.

Tip #18

Make sure your smoke tests on the live environment tests all integration 3rd party interfaces such as payment systems and email gateways. These interfaces are often hard to test in the reference environment and prone to errors due to wrong configurations.

Tip #19

Compile a list of improvements and send it to the sales team or customer sales contact for drumming up more business as change requests.

Tip #20

Track all defects that have been reported by users of the application. Although it is not possible to catch all defects before the software release ask yourself why did not catch these defects? Is it that your test cases were too narrow in scope? Or you did not have the appropriate testing equipment and platform to find this error. Plan to take steps in the future to cut done on defect leakage rate.

Tip #21

When there are too many bugs to fix before the release deadline hold bug triage meeting with the decision makers to review the open bugs list and choose which are most important bugs to fix before the release date.

Tip #22

Raise a ticket for all bugs found immediately no matter how minor the severity of the bug or unrelated to current testing task. The reason for this is that you may forget all the steps to create bug and lose the server logs of the bug. It might be harder to replicate the bug at a later time since you might forget what you did to reproduce the bug. If you have no time to report the ticket then take a screenshot of the page and copy the logs so that you can later view the context of the bug and recreate the bug.

Tip #23

Before doing a full live deployment consider doing a small dry run of the application using beta testers. A small pilot test run of the application for real user feedback and bugs reported by beta testers goes a long way to increasing the software quality of the product. Beta testing is highly recommended as a last line of defense against bugs.

Tip #24

Keep the test exit report short otherwise it won't be read. It should at a high level specify what has been tested and the results of the tests. It should indicate what known bugs have been found and not fixed.

Maintenance Testing

After the project is complete and the application is deployed maintenance testing starts. Here is where regression testing is needed to catch any bugs introduced as a result of new features or changes to existing features. It is best to have the same testers that tested the original release retest any new maintenance versions. The regression test suite should be updated once in a while so that it does not suffer the pesticide paradox of not finding new bugs with the same test cases over and over again.

Preventing Defects

Should tester promote preventing defects? Yes since it will make their job easier. Here is some advice to promote defect prevention.

- Hire better programmers that better code and replace the bad programmers that continue to code with lots of bugs.

- Use code reviews and requirements reviews.

- Write unit tests for the code and used code coverage tools to make sure you have good coverage with the unit tests.

- Write better requirements documents with lots of diagrams and examples.

- Use a software modelling language such as UML to specify the design. There are many other alternatives out there.

- Program in a language that prevents bugs from being created in the first place. Strongly typed languages give a level of protection that others do not. Languages that require all declarations to include specific data types, and that require *explicit* conversions catch a lot of errors that more permissive languages miss. Computer languages such as C and C++ that support arbitrary pointer arithmetic, casting, and deallocation are typically not memory safe and prone to security bugs and memory leaks.

⋏ Use software operating systems that are more reliable and secure. E.g. Linux

⋏ Use software frameworks and libraries that have few errors and easier to use.

⋏ Use static source code analyzer to parse the code and find bugs. Examples of source code analyzer are FindBugs (see Figure 14), Klocwork, Clang Static Analyzer, PMD, MOPS, and Coverity. A nice feature of FindBugs is that you do not need the source code to run an analysis of the code to find bugs since it works on a java jar file or Android apk file.

⋏ At the end of a project do a root analysis of the bugs reported. Based on this knowledge take steps to prevent bugs. For example if 6% of bugs are due to English errors ask developers to run the text descriptions in spelling, punctuation, and grammar checker.

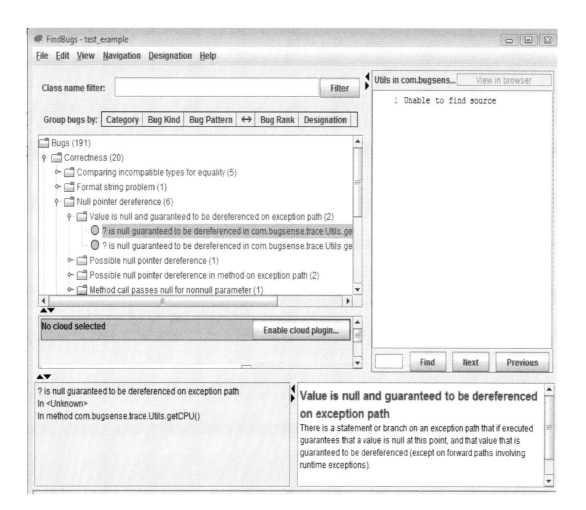

Figure 14

Chapter 12: Web App Testing

With the advent of the internet, web application testing is now a required skill of testers. Here is a list of software attack techniques to find bugs which can be used on web applications.

Broken Links Attack

Test that all the links on the page when clicked lead to a valid page and does not lead to a HTTP 404 error. Often a link crawler test app can be run to find all broken links automatically.

Bookmarked Link Attack

Test that bookmarked links when visited after re-opening the browser shows the page or redirects to the login page if user needs to be logged in to visit the page.

Back Button Attack

Test that pressing the browser's back button leads to the correct previous page. If a dialog is open it should be closed.

Refresh Button Attack

Test that pressing the browser's refresh button shows the same page over again updated with any changes from the server backend.

Resize Browser Attack

Test that resizing the browser to be smaller shows the elements on the back realigned properly. They should not overlap or crop each other. Text should not be missing and be nicely aligned.

Different Browser Attack

Test that the web app looks similar and works the same in all the browsers.

Tip #26

Use the free browser cloud-based service sandbox to test your application in different browsers. Spoon lets you run browsers directly from the Web without installing them on your PC. Spoon offers an impressive selection of the most current versions of Internet Explorer, Firefox, Safari, Chrome, and Opera on most any Windows-based computer.

Multiple Instances Attack

Test that the web app works properly when multiple instances are opened.

Hacked URL Attack

Test that the web app is able to handle URLs that are changed by a hacker. Get the URL of the web app from a network traffic monitoring app such a Fiddler. Then change the value after the = sign to a new value and see what happens.

E.g. param1=7 to param1=error

That is http://www.example.com/?param1=7&param2=seven

becomes http://www.example.com/?param1=error&param2=seven

Unencrypted Password Attack

Test that the web app does not send unencrypted passwords. Use the network traffic sniffer program such as Fiddler to view the request being sent has the password encrypted

SQL Injection Attack

Test the web app is immune against SQL injection attacks. What is SQL Injection? It is a trick to inject SQL query/command as an input possibly via web pages. Often web pages take parameters from web user, and make a SQL query to the database. For example when a user log ins, the login web page takes the user name and password and makes a SQL query to the database to check if the user has a valid name and password. With SQL Injection, it is possible for us to send crafted user name and/or password field that will change the SQL query and thus grant us something else. The best way to test if the webapp is not vulnerable to SQL injection is to run a test tool that does this testing automatically. Alternatively you can type in text fields sample SQL injection code such as the following: or 1=1

HTML JavaScript Injection Attack

Similarly to SQL injection test the web app is immune against

JavaScript injection attacks. Do this by submitting a form that is saved in a text field containing the following JavaScript

```
<script>alert('hello world');</script>
```

```
When the page is reopened with the page it will show
a JavaScript pop up with the test hello word. The
best way to test if the web app is vulnerable to
JavaScript injection is to run a test tool that does
this testing automatically.
```

Cookies Off/Javascript Off Attack

Test that the web app displays the correct error message when cookies or JavaScript is turned off if the web app requires them to be turned on in the browser settings.

Security Roles Attack

Test that the web app shows the correct pages for a given security role. For instance a standard user should not be able to see any pages that an administrator is able to view.

HTML Syntax Attack

Test that the HTML syntax of the pages are well formed. Use a HTML syntax tool to do this type of testing

Font Size Attack

Test that changing the text font in the browser shows the elements on the pages properly. Elements should not be missing or overlap other elements.

Spelling, Punctuation, and Grammar Attack

Test that the application is correct for spelling, punctuation, and grammar. Check the capitalization of the elements on the page. Microsoft's capitalization guideline has the following capitalization rules for the elements.

Title capitalization	Sentence capitalization
Button label	Check box label
Header	Combo box label
Menu label	Drop-down list items
Menu command label	Error message text
Option button label	Instructional text
Pop-up menu command	List box label
Split button label	Option button label
Soft key or touchable tile labels	Progress bar label
Tab label	Slider label

Text header	Text box label
Toolbar buttons	Drop-down list label
Screen tip	Text sub header
Tree view label	Time picker label
Window, dialog box, and error message titles	

Web Testing Non-Scripting Tools

There are some tests which tools at the click of a button or little prep work can save hours of manual testing or aid in testing without any programing. Here are some tests areas and the tools which help out:

- ⋏ Broken Links: Testing to see if there are any broken links in the website can be big job especially if the website is huge. It's better to have a web link validator (e.g. LinkChecker, see Figure 15) to do the job. Just enter the starting home page URL and press click. After a few minutes a full report will show the broken links with 404 error codes.

- ⋏ SQL Injection/XSS injection. Testing for SQL injection or cross site script injection in all fields can be daunting task. It is faster to run a SQL injection tester tool/XSS injection (e.g. Acunetix) and study the report afterwards

⋏ Spelling, Punctuation, and Grammar: All text needs to be read to make sure it has the correct spelling, punctuation and grammar and to see if it makes sense. However what if the tester is a poor speller or weak at punctuation and grammar? Here spellchecker tools are handy. Just the select text from the website and copy and paste the text into the MS Word and examine the red underscored words or sentences for errors.

⋏ Localization: Testing a web application that has been localized in another language which is not the tester's native language is difficult. Google's browser translation plug-in can save one from constantly checking a word in a dictionary to understand what's on the web page being tested.

⋏ Legal Compliance: Some of the tools cross scripting tools also have ability to check for compliance of the page for legal legislation and copyright law (e.g. SiteSort).

⋏ Accessibility: There are tools that check for accessibility compliance standards (e.g. SiteSort). Other tools even show how a website looks like to a color blind person (e.g. Vischeck).

⋏ Usability: There are many websites to help with usability testing to get feedback on a website or track user click movements on the website for analysis (e.g. Userlytics, Loop 11, FiveSecondTest).

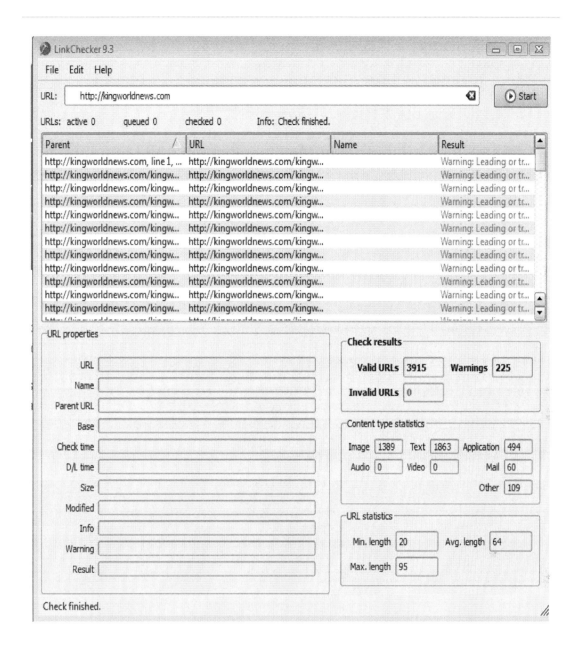

Figure 15

Top 10 Web Security Vulnerabilities

The Open Web Application Security Project (OWASP) is a global charitable organization focused on improving the security of software. Their mission is to make software security visible, so that individuals and organizations worldwide can make informed decisions about software security risks. Every year the OWASP organization publishes the top 10 2013 website vulnerabilities. Here is their list:

- A1-Injection - Injection flaws, such as SQL, OS, and LDAP injection occur when untrusted data is sent to an interpreter as part of a command or query.

- A2-Broken Authentication and Session Management - Authentication and session management are often not implemented correctly, allowing attackers to compromise passwords, or session tokens to assume other users' identities.

- A3-Cross-Site Scripting (XSS) - XSS flaws occur whenever an application takes untrusted data and sends it to a web browser without proper validation or escaping. XSS allows attackers to execute scripts in the victim's browser.

- A4-Insecure Direct Object References - A direct object reference occurs when a developer exposes a reference to an internal object, such as a file, directory, or database key. Without an access control check or other protection, attackers can manipulate these references to access unauthorized data.

- A5-Security Misconfiguration - Good security requires having a secure configuration defined and deployed for the application, frameworks servers, and platforms. Secure settings should be set instead of using the defaults which are often insecure. Additionally, software updated to the most current version which is patched to fix any existing security flaws.

- A6-Sensitive Data Exposure - A lot of web applications do not properly protect sensitive data, such as credit cards, tax IDs, and authentication credentials. Hackers may steal the data to perform crimes. Sensitive data needs to be encrypted for secure communication with the server.

⅄ A7-Missing Function Level Access Control - Applications need to perform the same access control check on the server as on the browser when each function is accessed. If requests are not verified, attackers will be able to forge unauthorized requests.

⅄ A8-Cross-Site Request Forgery - A CSRF attack forces a logged-on victim's browser to send a forged HTTP request, including the victim's session cookie and any other automatically included authentication information, to a vulnerable web application. This allows the hacker to force the victim's browser to send requests that the vulnerable application views as legitimate requests from the victim.

⅄ A9-Using Components with Known Vulnerabilities- Components, such as libraries and frameworks almost always run with full privileges. If a vulnerable component is exploited, such an attack can facilitate serious data loss or server takeover.

⅄ A10-Unvalidated Redirects and Forwards - Web applications can redirect victims to phishing or malware sites, or use forwards to access unauthorized pages.

Web Testing Security Tools

There are many security tools for testing web security which makes security testing easy. Next a sample of some of them:

⅄ Zed Attack Proxy (or ZAP for short). It automatically spiders a target URL and looks for common vulnerabilities, especially issues with cookies, headers and cross-scripting. See Figure 16.

⋏ One of the best SQL injection tools available today is a Firefox add-on called "SQL Inject Me" from Security Compass. See Figure 17.

⋏ WATOBO is an open source security tool maintained by an active community.

⋏ Qualsys's SSL Server Tester tests for basic quality issues such as whether your server supports SSL 2.0, which ciphers are supported, and the strength of your server certificate. It also tests more advanced quality measures such as whether or not client-initiated renegotiation is allowed and whether or not the BEAST attack would be mitigated.

⋏ Nikto is an Open Source (GPL) web server scanner which performs comprehensive tests against web servers for multiple items, including over 6400 potentially dangerous files/CGIs, checks for outdated versions of over 1200 servers, and version specific problems on over 270 servers. See Figure 18.

⋏ Netsparker is a web application security scanner, with support for both detection and exploitation of vulnerabilities. It aims to be false positive-free by only reporting confirmed vulnerabilities after successfully exploiting or otherwise testing them. See Figure 19.

⋏ Burp Suite is an integrated platform for attacking web applications. It contains a variety of tools with numerous interfaces between them designed to facilitate and speed up the process of attacking an application

⋏ W3af is an extremely popular, powerful, and flexible framework for finding and exploiting web application vulnerabilities. It is easy to use and extend and features dozens of plug-ins

- ⅄ Websecurify is a powerful web application security testing environment designed from the ground up to provide the best combination of automatic and manual vulnerability testing technologies

- ⅄ WebInspect is a web application security assessment tool that helps identify known and unknown vulnerabilities within the Web application layer. It can also help check that a Web server is configured properly, and attempts common web attacks such as parameter injection, cross-site scripting, directory traversal, and more.

- ⅄ Wapiti allows you to access the security of your web applications. It performs "black-box" scans looking for scripts and forms where it can inject data, like a fuzzer to see if a script is has security problems.

- ⅄ Suru is a web proxy fuzzer that sits between the browser and the web application. It receives all the requests made by a browser and records it. The requests can be modified in any way and replayed. Suru can fuzz any part of the HTTP request including GET and POST parameters.

Figure 16

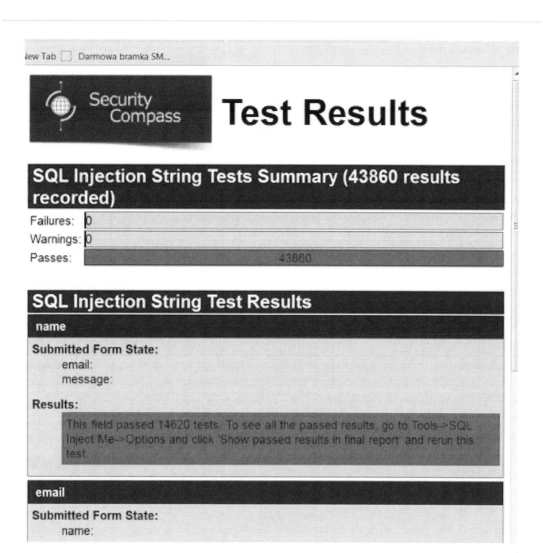

Figure 17

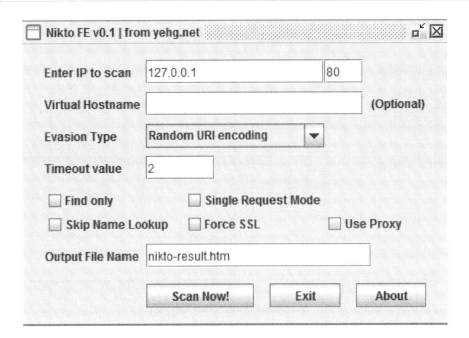

Figure 18

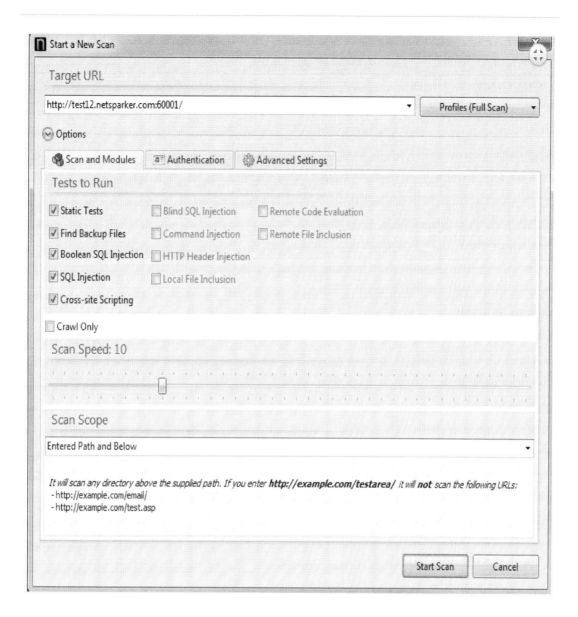

Figure 19

Chapter 13: Mobile App Testing

Mobile app testing is taking bigger role in the testing field due to the prevalence of mobile devices and the explosion of apps being built for them. Here is a list of software attack techniques to find bugs which can be used on mobile applications.

Interruption and Recovery Attack

Test that the application on the device is able to handle an interruption and recovery of a service. The different types of interruptions are:

- Incoming and outgoing SMS and MMS
- Incoming and outgoing calls
- Incoming notifications
- Battery removal
- Cable insertion and removal for data transfer
- Network outage and recovery for WiFi, GPRS, 2G, 3G, LTE
- Media player on/off
- Device power cycle (sleep mode)
- Home screen jump
- SIM card removal
- Clear application's data cache.
- Force stop and restart application.
- Switch to airplane mode

Tip #27

To test a loss of WiFi connection while the application is running, reverse tether the internet connection to your computer to the phone or tablet. This allows you to turn off the connection without turning off the router at any time from the computer to test how the app handles the loss of connection.

Installation Attack

Test that the installation, updating, and uninstallation of the application on the device is problem free from Google Play or Apple App store. If the application uses Google Play / Apple App store integration test that these services work.

Compatibility Attack

Test that the application is able to run on various platforms. Examples of this include different browsers, operating systems versions, and phones. Focus on the most popular phones and OS versions first and if time is available test on the less popular ones.

Screen Resolution Attack

Test the application on devices with different screen resolutions. Is the text font still readable at different resolutions?

Landscape/Portrait Orientation Attack

Test the application on devices works in landscape mode as well as portrait mode. Switch back and forth between the two orientations and check if the elements on the screen look right. Text and controls should not be truncated at the top, bottom and right side of the screen.

Usability Attack

Test that the application is easy-to-use and intuitive. Since a mobile device is smaller compared to a regular desktop computer, usability is very important to get right. Here are some guidelines that a mobile application should adhere to:

- ⅄ Keep the screen from being to information dense.
- ⅄ Controls should adhere to the OS design. E.g. back button is a physical button on Android at the bottom.
- ⅄ A welcome screen should be shown on starting the application or a tour screen.
- ⅄ Provide important content first.
- ⅄ Make tasks obvious.
- ⅄ For mobile website provide a fast download of the page with more simplified view so that the user does not to zoom in on the webpage.
- ⅄ There should be intuitive gestures used such as swipe to move to the next element or back to the previous element.
- ⅄ Use tips as necessary.
- ⅄ Use auto-complete and suggestions.
- ⅄ Use defaults for field values.
- ⅄ Make sure textboxes fits the screen
- ⅄ Allow for typos and abbreviations.
- ⅄ Include confirmation screens to prevent accidental changes.
- ⅄ First screen should be the main task screen from which other

screens are accessed with buttons for secondary tasks.

⋏ Use short clear labels.

Physical Keys Attack

Test the hardware keys work as they should for the application. For instance the dedicated camera button works for the camera application. Other examples are Task/Event Manager applications using hardware buttons to snooze a reminder, media players using volume and other keys etc. Some applications also use the power button to provide additional functionality / shortcuts to application behaviour.

Sensors Attack

Test the sensors work correctly for an application. For example test the GPS sensor for a GPS location based application. Other examples include applications that use the accelerometer such as games and jogging exercise apps. Test that the accelerometer sensor functions properly with these games and apps.

Security Attack

Test the application on devices is secure. For instance check the following:

⋏ Is your application storing payment information or credit card details?

⋏ Does your application use secure network protocols?

⋏ Can they be switched to insecure ones?

⋏ Does the application ask for more permissions than it needs?

⋏ Does the application use SSL certificates?

⋏ Does the application use a Device ID as an identifier?

⋏ Does the application require a user to be authenticated before they are allowed to access their data?

⚔ Is the username and password encrypted?

Use a mobile network proxy tool to re-route the traffic and check if the app's traffic is secure. Alternatively you can reverse engineer an Android apk file to get any hardcoded sensitive information using these steps:

1. Rename the file extension of the application from .apk extension to .zip

2. Unzip it and access all the app's resources and assets,

3. Use dex2jar to convert the class.dex files to a JAR file

4. Use a Java decompiler such as JD-GUI to access the source code from the JAR file.

5. From the obtained source code remove obfuscation, if present.

6. Study the code for hard coded sensitive information.

7. Report a security bug if such hard coded sensitive information is found.

Performance Attack

Test the application on devices runs fast, does not use too much memory, and does not drain the battery power life level too quickly. If the application connects to a backend server check how the server can handle heavy load with many client applications interacting with the server.

Payment/Ads/Social Media Integration Attack

Test that if the application makes use of in-app payment, advertisements or payment gateways for e-commerce transactions that it works. Check what happens if accounts are missing or they are network problems. Also test any social media integration with the application works properly to Facebook or Twitter.

Different Browsers Attack

Test the mobile web application on different default browsers on different devices including older OS versions.

Mobile Testing Tools

There a variety of testing tool available for testing a mobile application. Here are some tools useful for testing.

Emulators

All the popular phone platforms such as Android, iPhone, and Blackberry offer an emulator to develop and test your applications on a desktop computer without using a real phone. See Figure 20.

Pros:

- ⅄ No device is needed to test.

- ⅄ Different configuration profiles for resolution, memory, and other attributes can be setup and quickly tested.

- ⅄ Can test from your computer.

- ⅄ Can integrated easily with automation testing tools that run on the computer.

Cons:

- Not a real device hence defects might be missed which are only found a real hardware device.

- Game testing is not really possible.

- Takes time and skill to setup and run compared to a real phone.

- Slow to run compared to real smartphone. This can be helped by installing the Intel® Hardware Accelerated Execution Manager (Intel® HAXM), or KVM for Linux, to accelerate the Android Emulator by an order of magnitude.

- Sensor data, such as satellite location information, battery and power settings, and network connectivity, are all simulated using your computer.

- Phone calls cannot be placed or received but are simulated. SMS messages are also simulated and do not use a real network.

- Peripherals such as camera hardware are not fully functional.

- No USB or Bluetooth support is available.

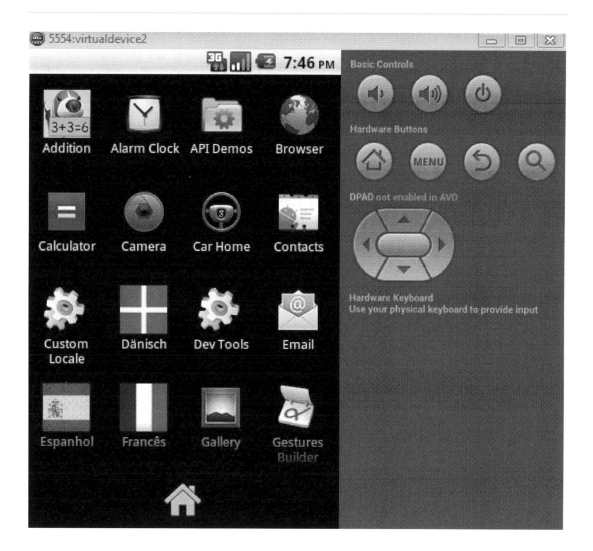

Figure 20

An alternative to using the Android emulator is Genymotion which is an emulator using x86 architecture virtualization, making it much more efficient. The emulator runs through Oracle's VM VirtualBox which takes advantage of OpenGL hardware acceleration which allows you to test your applications with amazing 3D performance. See Figure 21.

Figure 21

The Android emulator plugin can be used for continuous Jenkins build integration. It automates many Android development tasks including SDK installation, build file generation, emulator creation and launch, APK installation, monkey testing and analysis.

DeviceAnywhere

DeviceAnywhre is desktop platform that provides testing access to a huge variety of mobile devices. The specialty of the service is that they actually make use of a remote connection to real devices. See Figure 22.

Pros:

- lots of real devices to test on so you don't need to buy many new devices for testing.

- many different telecom networks around the globe for testing.

Cons:

- Slow response. After clicking on a button it takes a long time for a response. Hence this leads to frustration on the tester who thinks the app is not working and then clicks several times leading to navigation to unexpected screen.

- Popular devices are busy being used by other testers hence you need to wait to test on them.

- Other testers sometimes wreck the phone settings and setup which requires the phone to get reset by the support staff which takes time.

- Software on the devices is often outdated. This can be plus if looking to test with older software.

Figure 22

Paid alternatives to DeviceAnywhere with real devices include Perfecto Mobile, Xamarin and TestObject. Samsung Remote Test Lab allows you to test for free 30 minutes every day on their phones and tablets. Browserstack has a lot of different mobile emulators to test on for website testing. Other websites for mobile emulator testing include mobilephoneemulator.com (see Figure 23) and mobiletest.me

Figure 23

Testdroid

Testdroid is a test automation tool for Android and iOS devices. The toolset comes with recorder to create scripts which can be run as automated tests on real devices in the cloud. It can work with the following automated frameworks of Appium, Calabash, Robotium, Uiautomator, and Automation Instruments.

Intent Fuzzer

Intent Fuzzer is a tool by iSEC Partners, Inc. that can be used on any device Android OS device. Intent Fuzzer is a fuzzer. Fuzz testing or fuzzing is a technique used by hackers or testers to discover security loopholes in software, operating systems or networks by massive inputting of random data via data mutation or data generation, in an attempt to make it crash or unstable. The tool can either fuzz a single component or all components.

Monkey

Monkey is an Android testing fuzzer tool that executes on your emulator or device and generates pseudo-random streams of user events such as clicks, touches, swipes and system-level events. Hopper Test Tool does the same on a Windows Mobile phone.

MyMobiler

MyMobiler desktop application controls your Android device through USB connection or WiFi. It permits you to view your mobile device remotely and capture the screen or video. What you see in the desktop application is mirroring your device screen and you can interact with your device using the mouse and keyboard.

Pros:
- installation is easy.
- allows simple recording/taking screenshots.
- ability to use the keyboard (but not mouse) without rooting.

Cons:

⊥ unable to use the mouse without rooting.

⊥ slow (10 FPS).

An alternative to MyMobiler is Pocket Controller which must be purchased. It allows the tester via the desktop PC to quickly interact with an Android device to enter text and transfer data with no cables. See Figure 24.

Tip #28

Install Dropbox on each phone or tablet being used for testing so that screenshots taken on the device and be easily transferred to your computer to be added to the bug ticket report.

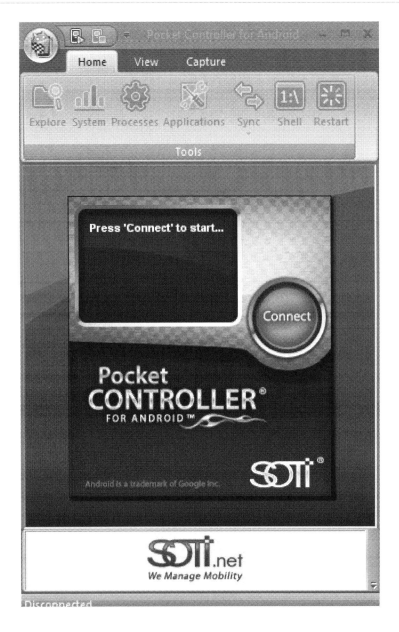

Figure 24

Unit Testing and Scripted UI Testing

Below are some testing tool for unit testing and scripted UI testing on mobile devices.

⋏ Robotium is a test automation framework for coding automatic black-box UI test scripts for Android applications. There is also a recorder that can be employed to record test scripts.

⋏ Xamarin is a test automation framework that uses NUnitLite which allows you to write unit tests against your Xamarin iOS & Android projects.

⅄ iOS testers can use either the older version OCUnit or the newer version of XCTest to write test scripts for iPhone and iPad.

⅄ UI Automator testing framework allows you to create automated functional UI test cases that can be executed against your app on one or more devices. See Figure 24.

⅄ Calabash gives testers the ability to write automated acceptance tests of mobile apps. Calabash is an open source cross-platform that supports Android and iOS apps,

⅄ Squish is the leading cross-platform/cross-technology GUI test automation tool for GUI regression tests on Android and iOS.

⅄ Ranorex supports recording and executing tests on actual mobile devices as well as on emulators without coding scripts. See Figure 25.

⅄ Appium is an open source test automation framework that tests iOS and Android apps using a webdriver. See Figure 26.

⅄ Perfecto Mobile's MobileCloud Automation is a cloud based solution for testing mobile apps on real devices and carriers. It exposes an API to better facilitate integration with continuous build tools.

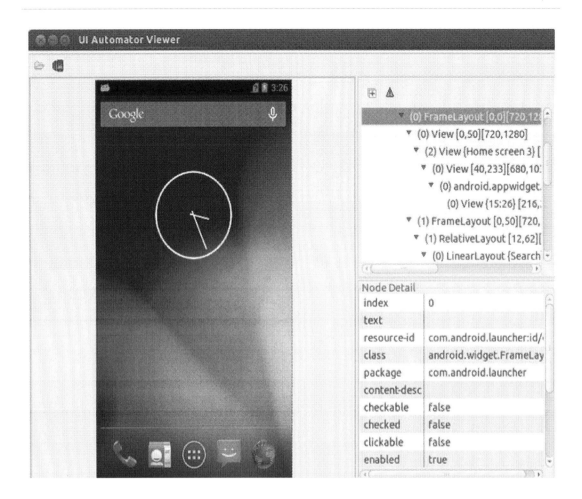

Figure 24

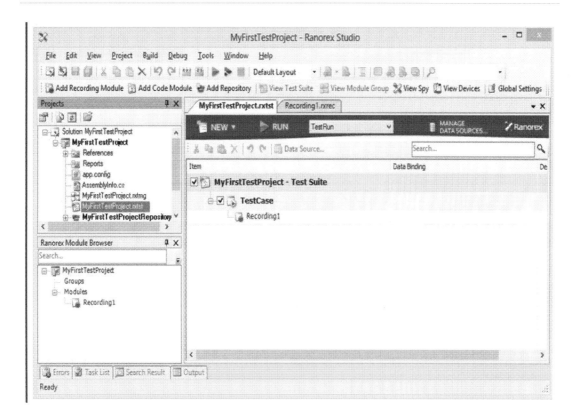

Figure 25

Figure 26

Mobile Security Testing Tools

Here is a list of mobile security tools mostly provided by iSEC Partners for testing apps available on Github.

- ⚑ Android-SSL-TrustKiller - This security tool hooks various methods in order to disable SSL certificate pinning, by forcing the

Android app to accept any SSL certificate.

⋏ Introspy for Android - Introspy for Android is a tool built for penetration testers to help understand the application's security mechanisms. See Figure 27.

⋏ iOS SSL Killswitch - One of the key tasks of the tester is to intercept the application's network communications using a proxy. This gives the tester the ability to observe how the application and the server communicate with each other. Successfully proxying the application's traffic can be challenging when the application uses SSL combined with certificate pinning in order to validate the server's identity. Without access to the application's source code to manually disable certificate validation, the tester is left with no easy options to intercept the app's traffic.

⋏ Manifest Explorer – It is a tool that can be used on any Android device. On Android, every application must have an AndroidManifest.xml file in its root directory. The AndroidManifest.xml file does a few things, which is all explained here. From a security perspective, the file is most interesting because it defines the permissions the application must have to other applications or protected parts of the API. The Manifest Explorer tool can be used to review the AndroidManifest.xml file, specifically the security permissions of the application, and the penetration tester a basic attack surface of the application. The attack surface is a critical starting point to understand security of the application and how it affects the mobile device itself.

⋏ Android SSL Bypass - It is an Android debugging tool that can be used for bypassing SSL verification on network connections, even when certificate pinning is implemented - as well as other debugging tasks. It runs as an interactive console.

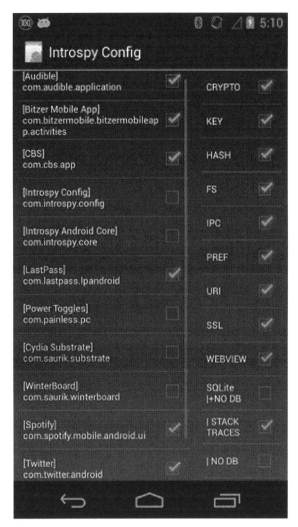

Figure 27

Chapter 14: Games Testing

Testing games is entirely different from websites, desktop or mobile phone apps. Besides being more fun, games require an entirely new approach. Here is a checklist to look for defects in testing multiplayer 3D games:

Scores Attack

Check the scores. Is the scoring right? Are the scores consistent between other players? Is the high score correct? Is it saved?

Avatar Profile Attack

Check the avatar's profile. After doing an action is the avatar's inventory showing the correct items, gold amount, level, number of lives, etc.?

Quest Log Attack

Check the quest log. Is it correct? Is it hard to understand or use?

Object Colliders Attack

Check the object colliders. Does the avatar's body go thru walls, fences, trees, etc. when it should not? Is the avatar movement stopped by invisible walls? Check for avatar floating effects by or on objects where the object colliders are not well defined.

Controls Attack

Check all the controls. What happens when you switch controls? What happens when you double click a button? What happens when you hold the controls down. Is the movement jerky? Does the player disappear underground on a mouse click movement?

Sounds Attack

Check the sounds. Are any missing? Do sound tracks start when they should? Do they end when they should? Is the volume right? Does the sound get louder on approaching the source?

Animations Attack

Check the animations. Are the animations visible by other avatars? Is it possible to start 2 animations are the same time which is not allowed? Are the animations smooth and realistic?

Edge of the World Attack

Check the edge of world. Can the avatar jump off the world? Can the player see past the edge of the world? Do rivers have bottoms?

Lags Attack

Check the lag in game. If the lag of the game is too long rubber banding or ghost effects can be seen with the player. Rubber banding happens when the avatar moves back to an old position like tied on a rubber band string. Ghosting happens when the avatar appears from nowhere like a ghost.

High Load Attack

Check how the game handles high load. Does the frames per rate drop too low when too many players are playing the game?

Memory Leaks Attack

Check for memory leaks of the game client console. Does the memory consumed continue to grow without any being released over X amount of play time?

Lost Connection Attack

Check how the game handles when the network connection is lost for networked games. Does the game hang? Is there feedback that there is a problem? Turn off the network connection while playing the game at different places of the game and observe what happens.

Other Players View Attack

Check the other players view. Does the other player see your animations, your scores, your chat, your change clothes or weapons? Two computers or tablets are required for testing this.

Light Effects Attack

Check for missing light effects. Are shadows missing for objects? Are reflections missing in windows, mirrors, rivers, etc.?

Water Effects Attack

Check for missing water effects. Does the water splash when jumped into? Is there a splash sound? Are there raindrops on puddles, rivers, etc.?

Proper Camera Action Attack

Check for proper camera action. Does the camera zoom in when getting close to an object? Does it zoom out when moving away from being close to an object?

Respawn Attack

Check the respawning and world entry mechanism. Does the observer avatar see the respawn point correctly? e.g. no floating.

Artificial Intelligence Attack

Check the artificial intelligence of computer opponents or non-person characters (NPC). Is the AI too dumb and makes too often bad moves for the hardness of the level? Conversely is the AI too smart and always wins for the hardness of level?

Spelling, Punctuation, and Grammar Attack

Check the spelling, grammar and punctuation in the NPC dialog.

Usability Attack

Check for the usability of the game. Is it too hard to see something or too many clicks are needed to do something. Is the color contrast good?

Artwork Attack

Check the artwork of the game. Does it match the design?

Mini Radar Maps Attack

Check the mini radar maps. Does it match what is seen on the big screen? Is too hard to understand?

Screen Resolution Attack

Check the game in various screen resolutions. Does the full screen view look like the other resolutions? Do the buttons show in the correct place? Is the text font crisp and clear? Is there too much lag at high resolutions?

Sky Attack

Check the sky. Does the sky look like a box around the world? Does the sun, moon, clouds move over time?

Weather Attack

Check the weather effects. Does the rain fall through roofs? Do the water bodies show raindrops as it rains? Do puddles form? Does the snow cover the objects as the snow fall continues over time? Does the trees, bushes and grass move when the wind blows? Is there lightning before the thunder sound?

Graphic Assets Attack

Check the loading of graphical assists bundles. Does it take too long to load the assists for the next scene? Are some assets missing? Or old assists cached and not refreshed with new asset changes?

Login/Logout Attack

What happens when you login on another browser or mobile phone? Does it show two avatars or prevent the second login? What happens when you quit mid game? Does it end the game properly?

Games Testing Tools

Lastly for games testing a video capture recording tool is a must in documenting certain type of bugs since screenshots are often not detailed enough to show defects with animations in the game. If a picture is worth a thousand words then a video is worth a million words.

A very good frames rate recording tool is FRAPS. See Figure 28.

For measuring lag consider using the tool Lagmeter by Bigfoot Networks. See Figure 29.

Use a network traffic monitor tool such as fiddler to check if the correct asset bundles are loaded. See Figure 30.

SyncTest is a nice tool for parallel testing of language localization of a game. It runs a master game on 1 computer say in English with the slave games in say German and French in 2 other computers. All games are viewable from one view.

Figure 28

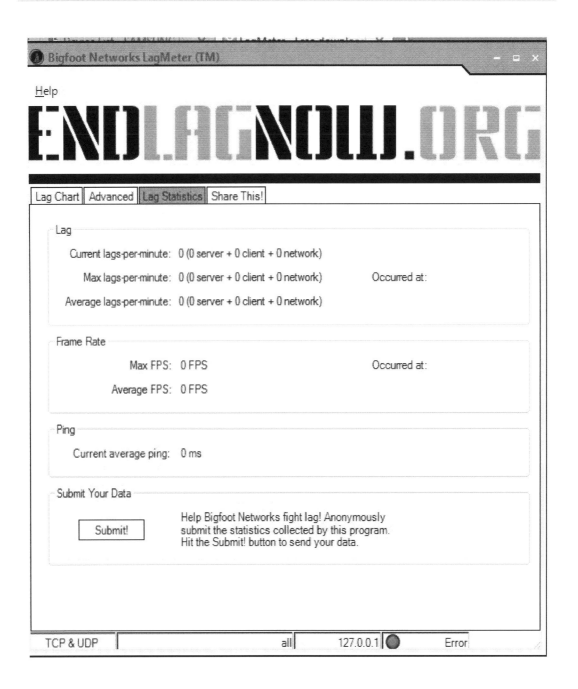

Figure 29

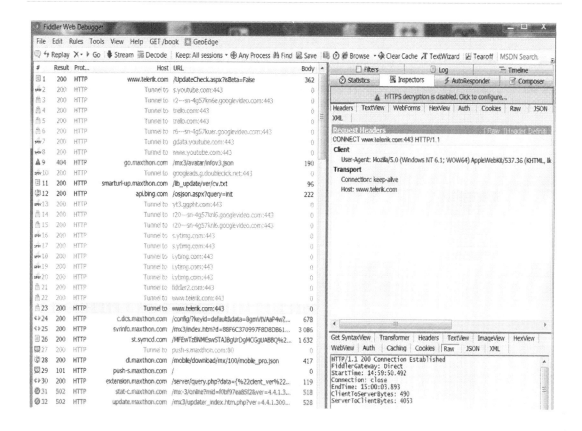

Figure 30.

Chapter 15: Performance Testing

Performance testing is conducted often at the end of development and testing to ensure that the system meets the performance requirements. Often performance testing is skipped in smaller companies or startups to save costs. This is mistake since there is high risk that that the system might perform poorly causing customers to stop using the application leading to loss of revenue.

Here is a list of different types of performance tests:

Load Testing

A load test is a test conducted to determine how the system will behave under a given load. The load usually is the number of concurrent users using the system at the same time performing a set of transactions over a set duration. This test provides the response times of the transactions. While doing load tests it is important to monitor the performance of the various components of the system such as the DB, application server CPU usage, free memory, file system i/o rates, network i/o rate, etc. to determine which component is the bottleneck in the system.

Tip #29

Make sure that the test tool generating the user requests load are on a different server other than the application server will the system under test is installed. Otherwise the test tool generating the requests will impact the results of the test.

Stress Testing

Stress testing is conducted to identify the maximum limits of system of when it breaks and how it breaks. Every system has a breaking point and knowing at what load it breaks helps the administrators react to when it reaches its breaking point. Also if the stress testing determines the maximum limit is too low then steps can be taken to improve this.

Tip #30

Double the user load after a successful test until the system breaks. If the system is able to handle 500 users then during the next time run with 1000 users. If that works then 2000 users. If that works then 5000 users. Once the stress test fails at say 2000 users then you know that the failure is between 1000 and 2000 users. Now you can test with half the value between the last interval, which is 1500 users. If that passes than again use half the interval between 1500 and 2000 and use 1750 users. Continue this method until the max limit is found.

Soak Testing

A soak test is an endurance test to determine if the system can maintain a continuous expected load over a time period. Memory utilization is monitored during the tests to find any memory leaks which typically reveal themselves over a long test. Also the throughput and average response time is monitored to make sure that the performance does not degrade over the test.

Spike Testing

A spike test is a test done with a sudden increase in the load on the system by a large amount and checking the behaviour of the system. The purpose of the test is to determine if the system is able to handle a huge jump of users on the system in a short time period.

Configuration Testing

Configuration testing is testing the performance of the system under various different configurations of the system to find the optimal setting. An example would be trying different indexes on DB tables or different number of worker threads reading off the job queue to find the best setting in terms of performance.

Performance Metrics

Below are some metrics to measure performance of a system or application.

Concurrency Users

If a system identifies end-users by some form of log-in procedure then a concurrency goal is highly desirable. By definition this is the largest number of concurrent system users that the system is expected to support at any given moment.

Throughput

Throughput is the amount of transactions produced over time during a test. It's also expressed as the amount of capacity that a website or application can handle. When presenting performance test results, throughput performance is often expressed as transactions per second or TPS.

Average Server Response Time

The average server response time is the average time it takes the server to respond to a request. For example this would be the response time for a HTTP 'GET' request from browser client to web server averaged over all requests. Most load testing tool measure this.

Error Rate

The error rate is the percentage of requests that result in errors on the request or response. This is usually happens when the system is under load.

Performance Testing Webapps and Mobile Apps

The following steps should be followed for performance testing:

1. Collect performance requirements. If the requirements are not specified in the original document ask the business analyst what they are. E.g. what is the maximum transaction per second of the system? What is the response time? How many users are expected to be handled? How much data will be in the database? Does the customer have sample test data?

2. Create performance test plan. Design tests based on the requirements. Identify the critical path user cases that need to be scripted.

3. Create test scripts and test data. The test scripts can be either

recorded or programmed. A large test data might also need to be generated with a customized program.

4. Setup test environment, monitoring tools, and test script executing tool.

5. Run tests and collect the results. Monitor the performance of the various components during the test to determine a bottleneck.

6. Analyse the results and raise defects. Check the logs for errors.

7. Programmers tune the code to fix the errors and clear any bottlenecks.

8. Re-run tests to retest fixes. Re-open tickets if still not fixed. Repeat step 7 and 8 until fixed. If the problem cannot be fixed by coding changes add more powerful hardware resources.

9. Write performance report.

Tip # 31

Testing a mobile app system which communicates with the backend server via web services is often simpler to test the backend server with a web services load client test tool such as JMeter or SOAPUI then with using real phone clients.   This simplification is justified since the bottleneck is often the backend server and not the client.

For mobile applications besides testing the backend performance it important the performance tests performance of the application on the device. This includes testing that the application on devices runs fast, does not use too much memory, and does not drain the battery power life level too quickly.

Performance Testing Games

The methodology for testing performance testing online games is similar as that for web app and mobile apps using a backend server. There are however a few differences which are the following:

- ⅄ Due to the sharing of other players' position and actions which can be a lot data if there are many players in the game, the client should be able handling updating the position of the other players' co-ordinates and actions quickly. Network traffic data needs to be optimized as much as possible. The frames rate will start to degrade dramatically when the client cannot handle the test load of the users.

- ⅄ Special scripts may be needed to generate fake bots on the server to simulate the user load while observing the performance characteristics on real game client for lag and frame rate. The path of the bots and actions should follow a typical path in the game instead of being randomized. Help will be required from the programmers to code this testing simulate bot tool.

Tip #32

Watch out for the test server generating client requests hitting the maximum CPU utilization limit of 100% while trying to stress the backend server to its maximum. If that occurs then another request test server needs to be added to the setup. Configure both generating requests test servers with original load split between them and continue ramping up the load until the backend server reaches its maximum performance.

Performance Testing Tools

Here is a list of some commonly used performance testing tools for measuring web application performance and load stress capacity. These load testing tools will ensure your application performs well in peak traffic and extreme stress conditions.

Opensource Performance Testing Tools

- Apache JMeter is a popular Java based performance testing tool for testing websites, mail services, web services, LDAP, database via JDBC, and TCP. It has a build in recorder to record web requests which can be parameterized. Test data can be read in from files or the DB to populate the parameters. See Figure 31.

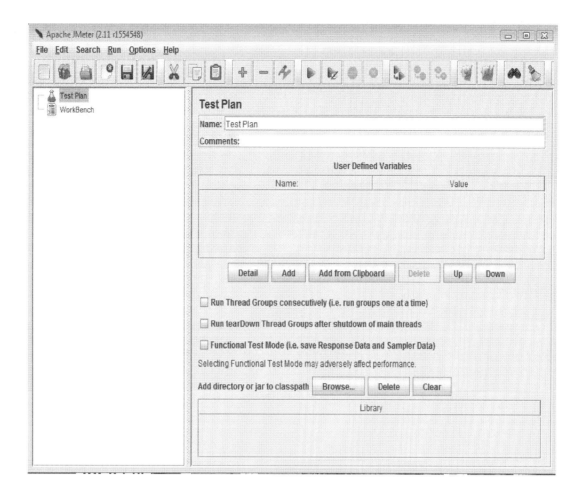

Figure 31

⚔ LoadUI is a graphical tool for load testing lots of protocols, such as Web Services, REST, AMF, JMS, JDBC as well as Web Sites. Tests can be distributed to any number of runners and be changed in real time. LoadUI is well integrated with soapUI.

.

⚔ The Grinder is a Java load-testing framework making it easy to orchestrate the activities of a test script in many processes across many machines, using a graphical console application. Test scripts are written using a dynamic scripting language like Jython.

⋏ OpenWebLoad is an easy-to-use tool for load testing web applications. It provides near real-time performance measurements of the application under test. OpenWebLoad is a command line tool that you execute from a command line like this:

```
openload [options] http://testapp.site.com 10

$ openload localhost 10
URL: http://localhost:80/
Clients: 10
MaTps 355.11, Tps 355.11, Resp Time   0.015, Err    0%, Count
511
     MaTps 339.50, Tps 199.00, Resp Time   0.051, Err    0%, Count
711
     MaTps 343.72, Tps 381.68, Resp Time   0.032, Err    0%, Count
1111
  MaTps 382.04, Tps 727.00, Resp Time  0.020, Err   0%, Count   1838
  MaTps 398.54, Tps 547.00, Resp Time  0.018, Err   0%, Count   2385
  MaTps 425.78, Tps 670.90, Resp Time  0.014, Err   0%, Count   3072


Total TPS: 452.90
Avg. Response time:  0.021 sec.
Max Response time:   0.769 sse
```

⋏ Tsung is an open-source multi-protocol distributed load testing tool. It can be used to load test servers running the following protocols: HTTP, WebDAV, SOAP, PostgreSQL, MySQL, LDAP and XMPP. The purpose of Tsung is to simulate users in order to test the scalability and performance of IP address based applications. See Figure 32.

⋏ Multi-Mechanize is an open source framework for web performance and load testing. It permits you to run simultaneous python scripts to generate load against a website or webservice

λ FunkLoad is a functional and load web tester, coded in Python, It does performance testing by loading the web application and monitoring your servers.

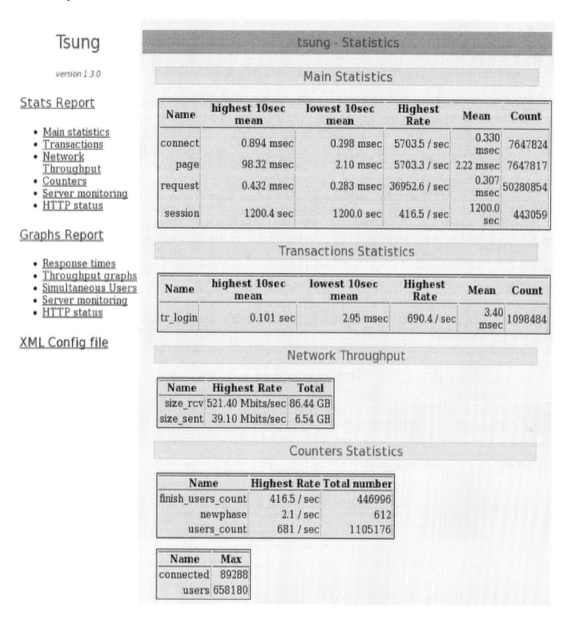

Figure 32

If you don't want to play around with setting up performance testing servers, installing performance tools on them, running tests and then generating reports, consider using these cloud based load testing services below. You may need to still create test scripts but at least you don't need to invest time and money on software and hardware for performance testing.

- ⚔ Load Impact is a leading online load testing service that lets you load test your website over the Internet. It's a pay-as-you-go on demand service, where you can start testing immediately and there are no licenses fees. See Figure 33.

- ⚔ CloudTest On-Demand simulates realistic conditions from thousands of local users to millions of concurrent and geographically dispersed users. CloudTest On-Demand allocates and provisions required the hardware resources quickly.

- ⚔ LoadStorm - A web-based load testing service that leverages the power of Amazon Web Services to scale on demand with processing power and bandwidth as needed. As the test loads increases to thousands of virtual users, LoadStorm automatically provisions more processing power from Amazon's server farm to handle the test load.

- ⚔ Neustar Web Performance - On-demand, self-service, pay-as-you-go service from Neustar enables simulation of large volumes of real browsers hitting a website. Utilizes Selenium. Uses cloud-based real or emulated browsers,

- ⚔ BlazeMeter's cloud load testing is equipped with an on-demand platform that uses JMeter and Selenium. BlazeMeter can run multiple load tests that easily simulate load of up to 300,000 concurrent users.

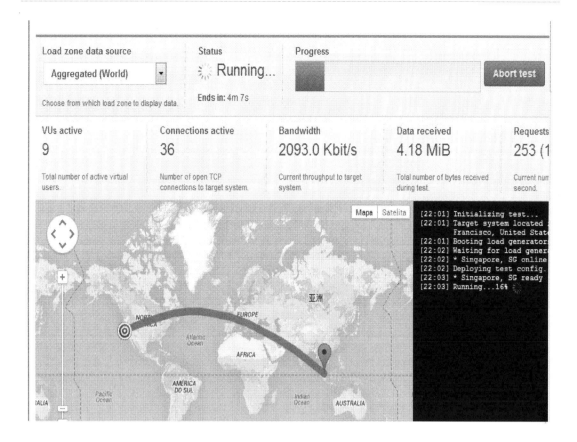

Figure 33

For mobile phones application performance testing there are many tools for testing battery life. CPU utilization, memory usage while your app is running. E.g. Nokia Energy Profiler. CPU Spy for Android, (see Figure 34) Battery Mix for Android (see Figure 35) Memory Status widget

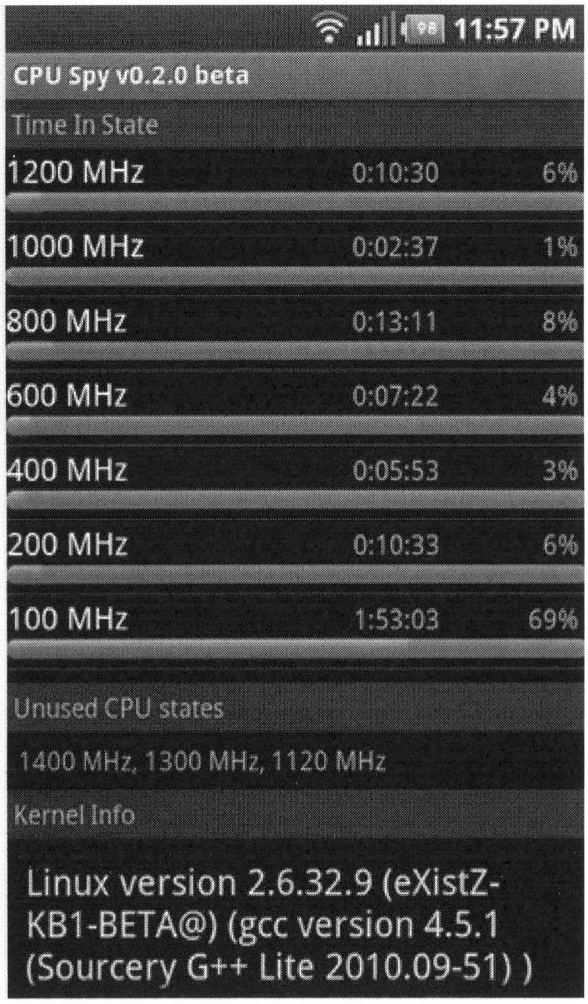
11:57 PM
CPU Spy v0.2.0 beta
Time In State
1200 MHz 0:10:30 6%
1000 MHz 0:02:37 1%
800 MHz 0:13:11 8%
600 MHz 0:07:22 4%
400 MHz 0:05:53 3%
200 MHz 0:10:33 6%
100 MHz 1:53:03 69%
Unused CPU states
1400 MHz, 1300 MHz, 1120 MHz
Kernel Info
Linux version 2.6.32.9 (eXistZ-KB1-BETA@) (gcc version 4.5.1 (Sourcery G++ Lite 2010.09-51))

Figure 34

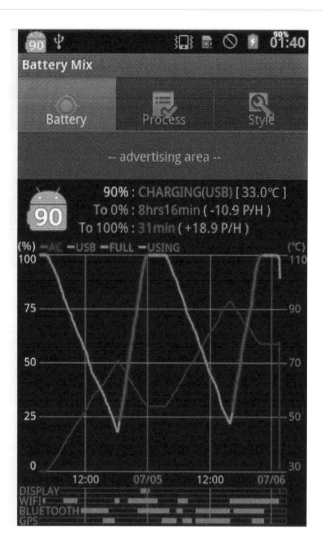

Figure 35

JMeter Testing

Below is a sample example of steps required for JMeter testing a customer service website on some Linux server boxes. The tool sar is monitor performance of various Linux subsystems (CPU, Memory, I/O..) in real time the output redirected to file for later analysis. For DB monitoring of MySQL use mytop which was inspired by top. The tool mytop will connect to a MySQL server and periodically run the *SHOW PROCESSLIST* and *SHOW STATUS* commands and attempt to summarize the information from them in a useful format.

1. Create a JMeter test script using the test script recorder in the visual JMeter tool workbench. The recorder is implemented as an HTTP(S) proxy server. You need to set up your browser use the proxy for all HTTP and HTTPS requests.

2. Optional: generate a test data file to be read to the JMeter test script .e.g. file of customer login usernames and passwords.

3. Install the JMeter script cust.jmx and test data file on the JMeter runner test box in the bin directory e.g. JMeter bin directory e.g. cd /home/runner/jmeter/apache-jmeter-2.7/bin

4. Update the user defined variables NUM_THREADS and NUM_LOOPS jmx files for that particular test.

5. On server box kick off sar cpu linux command in /home/mars/test with sar 5 1000 > sar_test1.txt

6. On DB mysql box kick off mytop a Mysql DB performance monitoring tool: `mytop -u username -p password -d database`

7. On server box for Customer execute the test script in the bin directory with ./jmeter -n -t /home/cust/jmeter/jmx/cust.jmx -l /cust/jmeter/logs/cust.jtl

8. Stop the sar logging with Control C when test ends.

9. Stop mytop with test ends.

10. Collect results from sar_test1.txt, grep logs for errors, etc.

11. Import the cust.jtl file into the JMeter tool to examine the errors.

Chapter 16: How to a Better Tester

Do you want to improve your testing skills? Here are some tips to take your abilities to the next level:

- Get certified as a software tester. The ISTQB organization offers a basic certification level and three advanced certifications for Test Manager, Test Analyst, and Technical Test Analyst. SQE. Besides looking good on your resume you will learn a lot about testing. You need to pass an exam to get certified after studying course materials. Ask your employer to cover the costs as part of the company's personal development plan. Here is a list of other tester certifications:

  - Certified Associate in Software Testing (CAST) offered by the QAI

  - CAT Certified Agile Tester offered by the *International Software Quality Institute*

  - CATe offered by the *International Institute for Software Testing*

  - Certified Manager in Software Testing (CMST) offered by the QAI

  - Certified Test Manager (CTM) offered by *International Institute for Software Testing*

  - Certified Software Tester (CSTE) offered by the Quality Assurance Institute (QAI)

- Certified Software Testing Manager (CSTM) by Global Association for Quality Management (GAQM) accredited via ASIC (Accreditation Services for International Colleges)a UK Govt. Accredited Body

- Post Graduate Diploma in Software and Mobile Testing (PGDSMT) by Global Association for Quality Management (GAQM)accredited via ASIC (Accreditation Services for International Colleges)a UK Govt. Accredited Body

- Certified Software Test Professional (CSTP) offered by the *International Institute for Software Testing*

- CSTP (TM) (Australian Version) offered by *K. J. Ross & Associates*

- ISEB offered by the Information Systems Examinations Board

- TMPF TMap Next Foundation offered by the *Examination Institute for Information Science*

- TMPA TMap Next Advanced offered by the *Examination Institute for Information Science*

- Attend tester conferences. There are many tester conferences held everywhere around the globe. Ask your employer to sponsor your trip to the conference early and get a discount on the entry free. If your company cannot afford the fee, then offer to be a presenter at the conference. Your ticket will be for free as a presenter. In Europe the EuroSTAR is the largest tester conference. In the US and Canada there are many tester conferences such as the ASTQB Software Testing Conference, QUEST test conference, STARCANADA and many others.

⚔ Read lots of testing books. This will give you new ideas to employ during your testing.

⚔ Attend tester club meetings in your city. This is a great way to meet other testers and learn from them by giving presentations. They are like mini-conferences on a local level held once a month. If you city does not have such a meeting for testers consider creating one. Approach your employer and pitch the idea to them to offer a room to hold the meeting.

⚔ Test new applications that are not related to the work for fun. Try to discover the bugs in these applications which the original testers of the application missed.

⚔ Read bug reports of good senior testers. This is a great way to pick up on new techniques.

⚔ Learn programming for writing automation scripts. Learn to write SQL so that you can query the database to see if the value entered in the application is correctly stored in the database. You attractiveness as an employee will increase as you will have a new useful skill.

⚔ Try new testing tools. Once you discover a great new tool introduce it to your tester team.

⚔ Try new testing methodologies like context driven testing, behaviour driven testing, and rapid testing.

⚔ Try as many combinations of data as fast as you can when testing. Testing is about trying to find the bug in the many data paths thru the code and the only way to find them is pumping the data thru the code by trying the software. Challenge yourself when you get to work to find a bug in the code in the first 5 minutes of work.

- ⚐ Improve your recognize differences skill. Do puzzles such as spot the differences between two pictures. A great website for such puzzles is www.SpotTheDifference.com. Jigsaw, crossword and word search puzzles (http://www.word-searches.org/) are also good for improving your critical observation skills.

- ⚐ Improve your written and spoken communication skills. Communication is a key skill for all testers since they need to inform developers about the bugs they need to fix and stakeholders about the status of the testing effort.

- ⚐ Hold a daily scrum with the developers to know what's coming down the next build pipeline and to ask questions about any problems or issues in need of clarification during testing. Also by holding joint scrum meetings it breaks the isolation between the testing and development teams. Testing and coding is not about rivalry but team work and by holding daily meetings you build bonds between the two teams into one team.

- ⚐ Be more critical. You job is to find problems and not agree with everything. However justify you critical viewpoints with strong logical arguments since you will need to backup your criticisms otherwise nobody will listen to you.

Time Management

Do you want to better than other testers and get pay raise? If yes then you need to learn good time management skills to get more done. Testers may have many activities to complete on potentially different projects so it's best to learn how to get the most done per day. Nobody likes working long days so learn to work efficiently with the time management tips below:

1. When testing new features, tackle the high priority/risk features first. Order you test plan's test cases by descending priority/risk to test the high priority/risk ones first. The same approach applies to retesting fixes. Test the blockers and criticals first, then the majors and finally the minors and trivials.

2. Put up a "Do not disturb" sign when you absolutely have to get work done. If you have an office room, close the door. If you have instant message change your status to busy or do not disturb.

3. Do not respond to emails when they show up. Better still close you email box so you don't even notice the arriving emails Schedule time to respond to email. Prioritize which emails to answer first and then let the low priority emails be answered the next day.

4. Do not answer phone calls when you are really busy. Let them go to voicemail to answer them later. Before getting back to a call take five minutes plan your response.

5. Take the first 10 minutes of every day to plan your day. Don't start your day until you complete your time plan.

6. If a conversation with a person is going to last a long time with lots of discussion it is better to schedule a meeting or even drop by the office of the person then using email, a phone call or instant messaging. Also remember body language accounts for 55% of the overall message which is missed using those other modes of communication.

7. Record important thoughts on notepad as quick to-do list so that you don't forget them.

8. Block out any distraction such as social media, internet, and music when you want to focus on completing an urgent task.

9. Schedule time for distractions like office hours to handle them on your terms.

10.   When reporting a bug, attach a screenshot to the ticket with the area of the app in which the bug is circled in red. Use paint or some other image editor to highlight the error. This will save time for the developer to understand what the error is. Remember a picture is worth a 1000 words so save time by using screenshots to quickly communicate the bug to the developer.

11.   Don't include long steps for recreating the bug in the bug ticket if the bug is obvious and can be explained with a short description and screenshot.

How to a Better Test Leader or Test Manager

Are you a test leader or inspire to become a test leader of a team of testers? Follow these tips on leading your team of testers to stellar results.

⚐ Invest in your tester's team education by buying tester books, paying for tester certification programs, and sending testers to conferences. Besides having smarter more educated testers as a result of educational investment the testers will be more loyal to the company. Do this especially if the developers get such treatment with trips to conferences otherwise you build up resentment in the tester team towards the development team.

- When selecting or hiring new testers to join your team, choose a tester whose skills will complement the existing members on the team. For instance pick a security tester to join a team that does not have a security tester. Or pick an automated tester for your team if the remaining members of the team are not strong as automating testers. This way you will get a stronger team and the members of the team will have chance to cross-train and learn new skills.

- Introduce new testing technologies and tools. Testers like to learn new techniques and new tools and get bored of doing the same thing the same way all the time. Add some variety to the tester's work. For instance if your company does no automation testing introduce this new technique to the company.

- Move testers around different testing projects so that they get bored testing the same product or type of application. Otherwise they might start looking for work at a different company to find that new and exciting feeling.

- Approve vacation requests as requested by testers if requested long in advance of project deadlines. Projects slip all the time so why punish a tester for the project manager's bad management of the project.

- Limit the tester's team overtime work otherwise it can lead to tester burnout. Pay the testers for their overtime work. If you cannot do that then at least order pizza for long testing days at work.

- Don't ask testers for daily email status reports. It more efficient to just hold a daily scrum with them to figure out what's going on the project.

- ⅄ Delegate testing work. You might be a super tester yourself but you cannot do all the testing yourself. Also monitor the delegated work to make sure it gets done.

- ⅄ Have other testers review your test plans, test estimates and test exit reports. This will catch errors and missing information from these documents.

- ⅄ Praise your testers for good work and criticize gently for bad work immediately. You don't want to wait for the end of year annual review to give feedback which affects the work being done today. Timely corrective action only happens when informed right away for bad work.

- ⅄ Fire lazy testers after a warning. There's plenty of eager hard working testers around so get rid of the lazy ones.

- ⅄ Check that not too many duplicate bug tickets are being reported. Too many duplicates is a sign of a tester being lazy and not searching the bug reporting tool before submitting a new ticket. Let the tester know that they need to check for duplicates.

- ⅄ Don't change the priority of a ticket without chatting with the reporter tester first otherwise they might get offended.

- ⅄ Don't close a ticket as invalid without justifying why it's invalid in the comments otherwise the reporter tester won't understand why it's invalid and might continue to report those types of errors in the future.

- ⅄ Be positive, professional, punctual and follow through and your commitments. Also never over commit to something if there is a good chance you cannot meet the commitment. If a commitment cannot be met due to some event beyond your control let the interested parties know about it advance. People don't like unpleasant surprises. Besides that, it gives the interest party an opportunity before it is too late to take steps to mitigate the failed commitment.

⅄ Hold a testing team improvement meeting every two months to get ideas from other testers on how to improve the testing process in the company.

⅄ Depending on the customer it sometimes best not to let them know of all the bugs found while the system is under development. Some customers do not understand that it is normal for lots of bugs to be found during the coding phase and react negatively at the knowledge of this. In this case it is best to have two bug tracking systems, one external bug tracker which shows any bugs found by the customer and another that is internally visible only to programmers, testers, and project managers.

Tester Relations

As a tester you will work with other members of the team such as developers, project managers, business analysts, software architects, customers, stake holders, and the deployment team. Testers have a unique role in that they are the critics of developers work. As such they need to be professional and objective. Testers play a support role to help developers in everything. Short of bringing coffee to developers testers should do whatever they are asked to do. If the developers want logs attached to bug tickets do so. Developers are not you enemy but your friend. You work for them. Hence do what they want. Do they need unit tests written? Do it if you have time after finishing your manual testing. Do they need the user manual written? Do it if there is nobody else available to write it. The developers need to concentrate on writing code and fixing bugs. You as a tester want to do your best to help them stay focused on that.

Tester needs to have a good communication contact with the developers. The testers and developers should have a daily short meeting together to keep each other informed of each other's work. This allows for issues brought up can be followed up quickly.

Tip #25

Don't re-open bug tickets that are closed by developers as "won't fix" unless the developer does not understand the severity of the problem. Re-open the ticket with a stronger argument saying why the bug should be fixed and provide solutions in the ticket on how to fix the problem. Alternatively go to the developer in person and discuss the issue. Sometimes a face-to-face talk is quicker to sort out an issue then playing ping-ping with a ticket back and forth between yourself and the developer.

For the project manager and stake holders as the test lead you will need to keep them informed of the progress of the testing. Once a week or per iteration an email needs to be sent to them informing the current testing status including the number of defects found, number closed, % of test cases of current test plan completed. Also what needs to be reported is the blocker tickets found and closed. Project managers will constantly hound you for updates on the testing progress hence they won't let you to forget about reporting the testing status.

For business analysts or customer you want to maintain a good relationship with them since they provide the requirements. If there is a question you just ask them. You also have to be diplomatic when pointing out logic errors and inconsistencies in the requirements. Also when there is a dispute between the developers and you over the validity of a bug you need to defer to the business analyst or customer to decide if the bug is correct or not.

Chapter 17: Future Trends in Testing

What's the future in testing looking like? There will be more automation and more social media testing. These are some possible trends in testing that the future holds:

- More crowd testing. With the advent of the internet connectivity it is now possible to hire a large set of tester on demand to run tests on your system. In the future crowd testing will be merged with crowd development and product owner will commission the whole development of the application.

- More automation automatically created from written requirements and formal models. With advances in artificial intelligence in natural language it will be possible for an AI agent to read the English requirements and automatically create test cases that will be executed automatically. Also as the software development process matures to using formal models of the requirements models like UML there will be more automated testing tools that will generate automated test cases from them.

A Integrated whole testing. Currently most tools are run individually. The future of testing will be integration of these different tools so that they can be chained together to provide a whole solution automatically. An example of this is the automated performance testing tool will be run after the security scanner tool.

A More self-reporting of bugs by the app with intelligent filtering of duplicates of issues. Some applications send bug reports when detected and log errors on the server. A common problem with this is bug reports that come back need to intelligently filtered so that the bug reported tool does not inundated with duplicates. Also these bugs need to be classified by severity and priority for repair intelligently. Again here some AI intelligence will be added to automate this task. Also there will be more incentives for users to report back bugs for cheaper less critical apps.

A More specialization of testers. Already the testing field has testers that specialize in automation testing, security testing, game testing, and usability testing. Besides specializing in testing techniques there will be specializing by industry. For instance testers will be specialized in business information for testing in the financial sector or specialized in medical information for testing in the medical manufacturing field. In the future testing teams will be composed of a team of specialist testers instead of a team of generalist testers.

A With the rise of globalism due to cheap network connectivity a tester team which would be co-located in the one location will be most likely be spread out around the globe and work as free lancers and assembled for the duration of the project. There will be tester work portals will keep tester profiles and allow testers to selected and assembled on the fly for a project.

⅄ Software programmers will become more testing and quality aware. They will be more conscious of how to code to prevent bugs. They will monitor their defect rate and take steps to reduce it. In order words, programmers will be become better quality minded professionals.

⅄ Virtual machines such as Oracle's VirtualBox will play a more important role in testing environment set up for different configurations. In the future when a defect is found the whole virtual machine with that current state of the machine will be packed up and emailed to the developer. This will better capture the defect state. Virtual machine recorders will capture snapshots of the events leading up to the defect making it easier to understand what caused the defect.

⅄ Security testing will take a more important role as companies begin to realize that their reputations are worth protecting from the risk of an embarrassing security breach found by hackers due to a lack of security testing.

Conclusion

Testing is a challenging activity which needs a special mind-set, skills and knowledge independent of the application being tested on. Becoming a champion tester requires an investment in time in learning new techniques and applying them. The world is full of software defects so don't delay and go find them with the tips, tools and attacks covered in this book.

Alphabetical   Index

37490353R00088

Printed in Great Britain
by Amazon